HOW A POEM CAN HAPPEN

How a Poem Can Happen

CONVERSATIONS WITH TWENTY-ONE
EXTRAORDINARY POETS

By Andrew Kuhn

FOREWORD BY
BILLY COLLINS

RED SPRUCE PRESS • • • NEW YORK

Published by Red Spruce Press

Copyright © 2017 by Andrew Kuhn.
Preface copyright © 2017 by Billy Collins
Afterword copyright © 2017 by Leisha Douglas

ISBN 978-0-692-87470-7

Library of Congress Control Number 2017939161

All permissions to reprint previously published material may be found on page 194.

Cover art: *Colloquial Humor* (2015) by Larry Wolhandler.
All photographs are by Leslye Smith except the following:
Photograph of Jill Bialosky by Joanne Chan.
Photograph of Aimee Nezhukumatathil by Dustin Parsons.
Photograph of Alan Shapiro by John Rosenthal.
Photograph of Christian Wiman by Danielle Chapman.
Design by Pamela Geismar, Domino Design.

Manufactured in the United States of America.

RED SPRUCE PRESS
Katonah, New York

For information on discounts for bulk orders, contact
katonahpoetry@gmail.com
For permissions, contact andrew@redsprucepress.com

FOR RACHEL, SAM AND THEO

"If you sat on the steps of the Katonah Village Library for the past fifty years without moving, you would have seen pretty much every major American poet walk through the doors."

Billy Collins, two-time United States Poet Laureate
Poetry Advisor, Katonah Poetry Series

CONTENTS

THE LIVELY ART
OF THE INTERVIEW

by Billy Collins

Whenever I happen to hear snippets of an entirely predictable late-night interview with a sitcom actor or a professional athlete, I wonder why anyone would think they'd have much of interest to say. Why should the ability to impersonate a suburban mom or throw a ball an astonishing distance bring with it a gift for putting unexpected things in interesting ways? In our celebrity culture, though, glamor is considered to make up for dull conversation.

It came as little surprise to me when Marlon Brando expressed his then scandalous opinion that most actors were not very smart. But authors, and specifically poets, are another matter. People who devote themselves to shaping language—and also, presumably, to habitual reading and critical thinking—ought to be interesting in conversation. If poets are really the unacknowledged legislators of the world who lift the veil from its hidden beauty, as Shelley believed, surely they should be found standing on the smart and articulate side of the line?

And some are—certainly all of the poets herein.

Of course, we can't expect a poet in interview mode to provide the same kind of pleasure as the poet does in a poem. And while a poet may provide context for specific works, it is a famously bad idea for an interviewer to request explanations. When Robert Frost was asked to demystify one of his poems after a public reading, he shot back: "Oh, you want me to say it *worse.*"

Perhaps by the same token, meeting the author in person is one of life's more reliably disappointing experiences. The writer's mask is there for a reason.

However, many poets prove quite nimble moving from the creative side of the brain to the analytic. Readers can easily forget that even poets spend most of their lives in prose. Seamus Heaney once reminded an interviewer that he was a poet only part of the time.

Writers who cross this bicameral border for the purposes of an interview are asked to engage in varieties of self-examination, which they may welcome, or not. A good interviewee can turn even an initially flat question into a fascinatingly faceted answer. Of course, writers are not necessarily more reliable narrators in interviews than in their literary works. Having to explain one's methods and motives can sometimes lead to inventing answers just for the sake of satisfying the questioner. Self-dramatization and self-deprecation are other available paths. Such misdirections may result in a more interesting interview than the mere facts would allow. The need to invent, whether due to imperfect memory or fear of discovery, can result in a mix of vivid though dubious fictions.

In spite of these complications, compelling truths do emerge. One need only look at the long tradition of *The Paris Review* interviews to see that close and informed literary questioning can not only trigger illuminating biographical admissions, but provide backstage access to the writer's imagination. I find this to be particularly true when the discussion turns to the subject of influence. There, we may discover the identities of the writer's literary parents—especially revealing if we somehow assumed the writer was an orphan. We often learn that what we naively mistook for utter originality was really an ability to brilliantly mix influences in ways too subtle for the sources to be detected.

Just the sound of a poet's colloquial, off-duty voice as he or she spontaneously fields a series of questions can deliver its own revelation. From reading the work of a poet, we may intimately know the persona—that constructed voice—the poet uses to address us, and on which we come to rely for its consistency. We may read a poet's work for insight, for the careful beauty of the language, and for imaginative epiphanies—for all of that and more. But we also turn to a favorite poet because we just want to hear that voice, that immediately recognizable, intimately familiar sound of the poet's language on the page silently heard in the reader's middle ear.

It's a little like the attachment, even affection, we have for a voice listened to regularly on the radio, issuing from a person we will probably never meet, may not even have a clue about what he or she looks like. What captures us is the sound itself.

So it's particularly interesting to discover how distant or close the poet's poetry voice is to the more casual voice used when answering questions. Sometimes they seem mystifyingly distant. Sometimes, though, the echoes of one in the other are unmistakable, to the extent that an answer to a question has the essential qualities of the poet's poetry. Broken into lines, given a title, an answer in conversation scans as a poem in itself. (Kuhn does it here, with Kay Ryan).

The interviewer's art is to bring to bear his or her knowledge of the poet's work and life in a way that provokes the poet into saying something unexpected. That takes preparation, timing, and the right amount of daring. Too little of the latter, and the reader gets predictable pabulum. Too much, and the poet takes offense and shuts it down. And quite rightly—just because you've put yourself out there in your poems doesn't make it open season on your past, present, and psyche.

For the most part—and I say this having experienced Kuhn's sometimes intense questions—he gets this balance right. He challenges his subjects, but from a place of deep sympathy and evident knowledge of what poets do, and the artistic choices they face. (The occasional humor doesn't hurt, either). The result for the poet is a bracing and ultimately pleasurable conversation about their life and craft; for the reader, a stream of vivid reminders about what is compelling about poetry, and an increased thirst to know more about these particular poets and their work.

Taken together, these interviews and the poems generously quoted with them provide a variety of unexpected perspectives on some remarkable poets' working lives, including their technique, compositional habits, obsessions, motives, and backgrounds. There are also some autobiographical surprises.

In looking at literature as a phenomenon, we distinguish between the writer and the work, even while retaining a sometimes guilty fascination with how the one relates to the other. These interviews allow us readers to enlarge our view of the poetry in light of a respectfully enhanced understanding of the poet's person and process.

• ● •

I have a vested interest in this collection. All of the subjects are poets who have appeared in the poetry series that has its home in the village library of Katonah, a leafy spot about an hour north of New York City. Launched in 1967, the Katonah Poetry Series is one of the longest-running poetry series in the New York metropolitan area. Mostly because I lived nearby and was asked by the series' founder, Robert Phillips, to do so, I took on the directorship of the series in the early 90s and kept at it for the next fifteen years. I still happily serve as consultant; my involvement continues to be an immense source of pleasure and satisfaction.

The series features four readers each year, and occasionally more. From its inception, all invited readers have been poets of the first magnitude, enjoying national reputations. The collection at hand offers an unusual opportunity to hear a diverse company of master practitioners reflecting on their craft, their development, and their lives.

WHY AND HOW
THIS BOOK CAME TO BE

by Andrew Kuhn

Why a book of poet interviews? Poems famously speak for themselves. Yet poems invite inquiry—demand it, even. And thankfully, not all poets stiff-arm their questioners. To an inquisitive reader who has dug into their work, many poets—the twenty-one represented in this volume among them—turn out to be astonishingly generous and forthcoming about matters of craft, influence, development, subject matter, tone, form, and even what they meant.

Such conversations don't stand in for or diminish the poems themselves, but add other dimensions and angles of view. One returns to the work with an enlarged appreciation for what goes into the making of specific poems, and insight into a particular poet's unique creative process.

This book had its genesis in 2010, with the efforts of a devoted group of community residents to put the Katonah Poetry Series on a firmer footing going forward. To help promote interest in upcoming poets, I suggested posting poet interviews on the Series website. In September 2011, I interviewed Aimee Nezhukumatathil, commencing what has now become a KPS tradition.

Preparing for these exchanges has afforded me the opportunity to dig into and appreciate the work of masterful poets in ways I never would have done otherwise. That labor made its own rewards, as I'd imagined it might. What I didn't anticipate was the generosity of the poets and their openness to entering into dialogue with a stranger, and to answering at times challenging (impertinent?) questions.

Over time, I became freer in my questioning. I reasoned, or rationalized, that writers put a lot of who they are into the public realm, so that issues and matters they've raised in print are fair game to ask about, in a respectful and tactful sort of way. And anyway, writers are grown-ups; if they don't want to answer something, they don't have to, as I emphasized to them in my introductory emails. Nevertheless, few declined to answer even one of my questions.

Being free to imagine an audience for these posts was liberating. I posited an informed and engaged readership with a robust attention span, and a willingness to tolerate this questioner's sometimes baroque grammatical constructions. The community has been kind enough not to disabuse me of these reveries.

It may or may not be a coincidence that my progress towards a more direct or intrusive style of questioning in the interviews paralleled my development over a longer period as a psychologist (my day job). Having started with a strict shrink-be-quiet psychoanalytic orientation, I progressed over time to a more actively inquisitive stance. Whether that represented a return of the repressed journalist I'd been many years back, who knows; a lot of therapists have followed the same arc over time in their everyday work. In any case, these literary conversations have been far more gratifying than I had any right to expect.

I am grateful to the poets for affording me the opportunity to share the delight I experienced in encountering their poems, and their thoughts about their work, in a spirit of mutual inquiry. The purpose of this book is to widen that circle of delight to include other passionate readers and writers of poetry.

INTERVIEWS

MARY JO BANG

• • •

Mary Jo Bang has had a protean succession of occupations—sociologist, photographer, physician's assistant, professor—excelled only by the shape-shifting (and tone- and technique-shifting) range of her poetry. Her collection *Apology for Want* (1997) was awarded the Katherine Bakeless Nason Prize; *Elegy* (2007) won both the National Book Critics Circle Award and the Alice Fay di Castagnola Award. Other collections include *The Bride of E* (2009), *Louise in Love* (2001), and *The Downstream Extremity of the Isle of Swans* (2001). The editor of *The Boston Review* from 1995–2005, she won the *Discovery / The Nation* prize, as well as fellowships from Princeton and both the Guggenheim and Bellagio foundations.

Bang's poetry has appeared in *The New Yorker*, *New Republic*, *Kenyon Review*, *Yale Review* and *The Paris Review*. In her poems she has conjured with art, history, popular culture and its history, post-post-modernism, and searing personal loss, in ways that blend and bend poetic genres and modes of address. About her collection *The Last Two Seconds* (2015), *Publisher's Weekly* wrote in a starred review: "A powerful, caustic set of lyrical and antilyrical works. . . . Attentive readers who delve into Bang's sharply articulated vision will find them unforgiving indeed—and those same readers will praise her to the skies."

KPS READING: MAY 2016

Andrew Kuhn: You are not only the most extensively and variously educated poet I've ever come across, but probably one of the most degreed human beings of any description. Can you say a little about how your vigorous pursuit of such varied disciplines as photography and medicine informed your engagement with poetry and the problems posed in making it?

Mary Jo Bang: I'm afraid you are overstating the extent (and degreeness) of my education, especially since I have no Ph.D. There are many poets with advanced degrees, and possibly some with both Ph.D.s and M.D.s. That said, in terms of my educational forays, I do think the thoroughness with which one ends up investigating a subject in a degree program (or in the case of my medical training, a certificate program—I was a Physician Assistant, not a doctor), allows a person to gain a certain level of mastery and an appreciation for the vastness of the subject. I will never know as much as I want to know about poetry but I keep getting smarter about the craft of it, about my own psychic merger with it, and about the possible mindset of those who wrote verse in the past. All of that was equally true for me when I studied photography.

AK: There are poets who write sentences that wouldn't necessarily seem like poetry except that they are arranged on the page in a raggedy fashion, and that the writers are known to be poets. What you write, on the other hand, could be nothing but poetry. Its discontinuities, lateral leaps, serene and emphatic improbabilities maintain that poetic discourse is unique and will make and break its own rules, thank you very much.

Do you think that the advent of "accessible" poets and poetry, while they widen the audience for poetry in general, poses problems, and may even represent a threat for the survival of poetry as a unique and vibrant literary enterprise?

MJB: I don't think poetry is threatened by anything. I think poetry's greatest strength is that one can do with it whatever one wants to.

Because of that, I would never suggest placing limits on it. I learn from everything I read. Occasionally the lesson is how to avoid doing in my own work what I find a poet doing in work that I don't enjoy reading.

AK: With the exception of the collection *Elegy* (Graywolf, 2007), which charts the year after the death of your son, you have rigorously declined to be "confessional" in your poetry. You've referred elsewhere to the exhaustion of "the romantic poetry notion that I stand at the center of the world and I can speak for you, because I know how things are." If the platform of confident subjectivity is denied to or abjured by the poet, though, what's left to stand on? The tragicomedy of falling-in-place has been fruitful for everything from Beckett's works to "Road Runner" cartoons, and your own work is full of trapdoors. Still, is there a danger that poetry will wear out the trope and, eventually, itself?

MJB: I worry that you might be confusing "non-confessional" poetry with an un-embodied poetry. As Eliot taught us (in "Tradition and the Individual Talent"), impersonality on the page is the very thing that allows the emotional poet to escape those particulars that are most mentally abrasive (a temporary escape through the distraction of creating, which is more than a bit like falling down Alice's rabbit hole and staying busy tracking Cheshire cats that appear and disappear). However, we never escape our own subjectivity. It gets written into every word we write.

AK: Your volume *Louise in Love* (Grove Press, 2001) could be seen as representing an interesting work-around for the problem of romance and subjectivity, and maybe provides evidence that you're not quite finished with the Romantic project. Here, it is not the poet (or the poet's persona) speaking in all naïve (or faux-naif) sincerity. All of the poems are from the point of view of a character who bears similarities to the Louise Brooks pictured on the cover, the film actress and dancer who seemed to embody the louche glamor of the Twenties.

This double-distancing of person and time allows for some quite lively and at times erotic subjectivity. But her take on love is mordant, to say the least. "Captivity" opens like this:

> Those birds will eat anything—
> The carcass subsumed in death, the heart convulsing
> In laughter. So this is how it ends, a dart in the eye
> Of Ifdom. The duck grows
> Up to be a pillow, the table takes the tree
> Out for a talk—We must stop meeting like this.

What's all this got to do with love? We find out a few lines later.

> That kind of desolation can double as solace, Louise said.
> Yes, the skeleton dreaming its body back to a particular
> Limit—a lovely skin, a mind that knows nothing
> Of boundaries, the erotic singsong of motion.
> The happy little cage.

How did Louise Brooks become a muse for you, if that's a fair way of putting it? You started as a writer of short stories. After *Louise in Love*, have you been tempted again to re-claim for poetry the right to write from others' points of view?

MB: *Louise in Love* began on a solo visit to an early NYC Starbucks coffee shop. While sitting there alone (circa 1995), I had a silent conversation with two imaginary friends—a conversation partially fueled by the memory of the tortured love-triangle in Truffaut's *Jules and Jim*. That day in Starbucks, I invented a female character named Louise, a man named Ham (short for Hamilton), and I imagined a third, unnamed and un-gendered, character that I referred to in the poem as "the other."

Later, I found a postcard of Louise Brooks in a shoebox full of ephemera I had collected during my years in London and realized that my Louise looked just like Louise Brooks. I then read a biography of Brooks, and her own book, *Lulu in Hollywood*, and appropriated a bit of the language and some of the circumstances. But I always knew that while my Louise might look like Louise Brooks, and might some-times act like Brooks—in both her films and in her real life—she wasn't Brooks. She was her own person—a full-blown figment of my imagi-nation.

In terms of the temptation to again use a real-life figure as the basis of invention, I've just finished a new collection of poems where I've used the Bauhaus photographer Lucia Moholy in a similar way. There is one continuous speaker for all of the poems, a woman who is part Moholy, part me, and part pure invention. (That collection is called *A Doll for Throwing* and will be published in August of 2017.)

AK: Not many poets mention Freud at all in their work, but there are a surprising number of references to him in yours. HD (Hilda Doolittle) was a patient of Freud's and a poet of note at the time, but many liter-ary artists seem to feel that Freud and his descendants are kryptonite for creativity. Could you say a little about how your encounters with Freud and his works (and/or workers) have influenced your develop-ment as a person and a poet?

MJB: Freud has meant a great deal to me. I first opened *The Interpre-tation of Dreams* when I was thirteen. That was when the books that were kept in a glass-enclosed room behind the reference counter at the local library became available. You couldn't take those books home but anyone thirteen or older could sit at a table and read one of them. I looked through the card catalogue and was intrigued by the title of that one and asked for it. I then sat at the table and read it for hours. I found it both fantastical, and fascinating.

Over my lifetime, I've read most of what Freud wrote, as well as several biographies. I think he's a very important figure, limited by his historical moment, and by his egotism, but who isn't. He got some things right and he spoke openly about many things that others were silent about. Especially in the realm of sexuality. I take what I want from him, and leave the rest.

AK: The abstemiousness of your poetry can be quite striking. At times it seems that you not only don't care to be understood too easily, but are vigilant against such a danger, to the extent that the poems have a certain unyielding quality, a steeliness. The reader is challenged not just to meet you half way, but to swim a cold river to reach you on the far side; and the sense is, whether we make it or not, that's our look-out. Take, for instance, the opening of "M As In Masks":

> The psychic investiture of a seal, an impression
> Badly done of some other who presented
> One morning as a caricature
> Of a crying doll in a cradle with Freud leaning over
> A mirror and seeing only the bottom of his beard.

Is it unfair to ask, where are we? Who's being addressed about what, in particular? The combination of specificity and abstraction, the arabesques of syntax without a unifying subject or verb, are disorienting, a sort of linguistic hall of mirrors. Even the modest semantic hinges we tend to rely on to show us how one part of an utterance and another might be linked—here, "with"—turn out to be unreliable. We think Freud's leaning over a crying doll in a cradle, but no, it's a mirror he's leaning over . . . so is the mirror in the cradle too? Nothing so literal as that, most likely. Still, one way and another, in five lines, we've already had quite a workout.

Do you have a clear sense of what you'd like your readers to make of any specific poem? Or is that not a major concern for you, and the question poorly conceived?

MJB: For me, every poem is about consciousness. Primarily mine, but also consciousness as I understand it from what I've read and from what I've seen in a lifetime of observing others. What the reader is being offered when they read a poem written by me is the movie of my mind, but in flux. The film has to be in flux because the mind is not only multi-layered but also dynamic. If you limit yourself to language to represent a fluid mind—then, of course, the representation will be inexact, abbreviated, and it might sometimes seem chaotic, or at the very least acrobatic.

In order to better represent "what I mean," in the poem, I try to exploit the sounds inherent in language, as well as the fused layers of meaning that accompany sound (sonically, for instance, *tail* evokes *tale* if you put it near the word *fairy*). But no matter what I do with language, I can't open the cabinet door and allow the reader to see everything that is in that overstuffed Fibber McGee-ish closet that is my mind.

That's the problem, isn't it? No one *can* completely know the mind of another. Which is both isolating, and consoling. At best, the poem is gestural. I try to create gestures that will evoke both a subjectivity and a visual world that stands for thoughts.

Do you know Oscar Schlemmer's Bauhaus dances? I see the poem as a bit like that. It's both serious and playful and it uses dolls as figures in space. The dolls make gestures and as they do, they become gestures. The meaning of the gestures depends on the viewer's perception. In that way, watching becomes part of the dance. Transferring that notion to poetry, reading becomes part of the movie.

AK: I do not know Oscar Schlemmer, but I will look him up . . . You spent some years that seem to have been quite important—in terms of your development—out of the country, primarily in England. My impression, partly from other conversations you've shared, is that this was during the hegemonic heyday of the European semioticians and deconstructionists, and that you took these thinkers on in a thorough-going way. That can be a heavy legacy to work through, for an artist.

Did the post-everything perspective of some of these thinkers have an inhibiting effect on your poetic impulses at the time? Or has your poetry only profited by your having metabolized these influences?

MJB: My first impulse was to say that I've never been inhibited by the thinking of others but then I immediately realized how patently untrue that is. I think the truth is that I'm continually inhibited, but since I hate being inhibited, to deal with that state, I seek permission—

sometimes by reading more deeply, sometimes by looking at the example of others who are less inhibited.

Hopkins, for instance, can give permission of one sort; Stein, permission of another sort. I often go to the visual arts to be reminded of how little narrative it takes to evoke a world, and how a blotch of color can evoke more emotion than an entire novel.

AK: Your poetry is notably short on Americana, certainly of the amber-waves-of-grain variety, or even specific identifiable locations. Iconic pop references do crop up (cartoon characters, notably). In the mordantly titled "U Is For United," however, you almost casually confront a major tension at the heart of the American project, opening with:

> The contrast with liberty is striking: impediment,
> Impediment, impediment.
> What sort of guarantee is that?
> My x-ray heart, stark against the light box of servitude.

The poem concludes about as darkly as could be:

> Yes, I know, the gold star is tarnished in the cap
> On the coffin lid. An oil-spill iridescence
> Catches the dying light. "Sorry," says Cerberus,
> Each mouth moving in unison.

Did your time away from the U.S. help to make what I can't believe it's now conventional to call the Homeland enduringly strange, in a way that's fruitful in terms of engaging it poetically, at a slant? Is it difficult to write poetry that is politically oriented or engaged that is also uncompromised as poetry?

MJB: That's so funny that you find very little of America in my poems! I think my poems are quintessentially American. I think my humor is American. I think my poetics are a marriage of Whitman and Dickinson (perhaps with Eliot and Stein arm wrestling in the background). In terms of "politics," I think everything I write is political although in the narrowest sense of that word, the poems in my most recent book,

The Last Two Seconds (Graywolf Press, 2015), are the most explicitly so. The political impulse that is consistent throughout my work is a lament over the real damage done by rigid thinking, and over the limitations placed on personal freedom. I think in the past, sometimes the poems enacted the struggle instead of speaking about it.

AK: Looking over the list of past readers for the Katonah Poetry Series, are there poets who have influenced your own development?

MJB: Many of those poets have influenced me, each in his or her own way. Tate, Swenson, and Rich stand out among those who are gone. Lucie Brock-Broido was my teacher during the time when I first began to write. Her influence is significant and ongoing. And I'm influenced by all of those still living. I read widely and learn from whatever I read.

• ● •

ELLEN BASS

• ● •

Ellen Bass combines a passionate engagement with issues of justice and human rights with a pitch-perfect poetic ear. Her poems are generous, flexible, fresh, free of cant, and mordantly funny. Honors include a National Endowment for the Arts fellowship, the Pablo Neruda Prize, and many others. Her work has appeared in *The New Yorker*, *The Atlantic*, *The New Republic*, *Ploughshares*, *Kenyon Review*, and *The New York Times Magazine*. Collections include *Like A Beggar*, *The Human Line*, and *Mules of Love*. Bass has also written influential non-fiction books. First published in 1988, *The Courage to Heal: A Guide for Women Survivors of Child Sexual Abuse* (Harper Collins), has sold over a million copies and been translated into ten languages. Ellen Bass also has an acute and welcoming approach as a teacher, as those who have been fortunate enough to work with her will tell you.

From a review in *Lilith*: "Bass builds the epic from the ordinary and celebrates the ordinary as exceptional. Filled with odes and lyrical, prayer-like meditations, *Like a Beggar* 'love[s] the truth.' In the first poem 'Relax,' Bass warned, 'Bad things are going to happen;' and they do, in this book, in life, but Bass renders them livable and beautiful. . . . *Like a Beggar* is an exuberant celebration of living in the world."

KPS READING: SEPTEMBER 2014

Andrew Kuhn: Has anyone ever used the word "swashbuckling" in connection with your poetry? Would you mind very much if they did?

Ellen Bass: Swashbuckling! This is definitely the first time. I'm sure I'd remember it if they did. But how could I not be delighted to have my poems thought of as daring and heroic and a bit flamboyant!

AK: Some poets don't let us know very much about their personal histories, lives, relations; others do. It seems fair to place you in the latter camp. While many personal or "confessional" poets dwell in particular on dark histories and develop a rhetoric of personal despair (Sylvia Plath, Anne Sexton, Robert Lowell), you often acknowledge dark matters but eschew despair. Have you experienced that there can be some resistance, when your writing is hopeful or even exuberant, to being taken entirely seriously as a poet?

EB: Maybe I can answer this question in two parts. First, I do mine my personal experience in the making of poems. But that experience is not the story of my life. It's the material available to me to use. It's like scraps of cloth. But then I have to make the quilt. I have to decide the pattern and the colors and the way the pieces will be stitched together.

There are elements in my poems that come from my life and there are elements that come from other people's lives. Often they're presented in ways that are indistinguishable. I think of what Orhan Pamuk said, that the writer "must have the artistry to tell his own stories as if they were other people's stories, and to tell other people's stories as if they were his own, for that is what literature is." That's what I aspire to.

As for my insistence on joy, the great poet Lucille Clifton said, "I choose joy because I am capable of it, and there are those who are not." She was no stranger to suffering. She lived through the deaths of two children and her husband, her own cancer and other illnesses. I don't think that joy is incompatible with seriousness. The Tibetan Buddhist teacher Chogyam Trungpa Rinpoche said, "If you can hold the pain of the world in your heart but never forget the vastness of the great eastern sun, then you can make a proper cup of tea." And I quote Rilke for the epigraph in my recent book, *Like a Beggar* (Copper Canyon Press, 2015): "But those dark, deadly, devastating ways,/how do you bear them, suffer them?/–I praise."

AK: Among your extraordinary poems is "Worry," which manages to convey in a few pages a multi-generational history of trauma in almost conversational language that is anything but overwrought. These are the final two stanzas:

> And in Russia—my father was a baby
> when his mother carried him and two brothers
> to the border. Hiding
> in the forest undergrowth, my father
> crying, she heard boots
> bite through the crusted snow. Some women
> smothered infants. What must have gone
> through her mind when the steps hesitated,
> before turning away?
>
> Janet doesn't think about what
> might happen. She thinks about what is.
> But I carry dread on my shoulders
> like a knapsack, like the extra pounds
> my grandmother wanted me to gain.
> She'd read about a girl in a plane crash.
> All she had to eat was snow.
>
> [From *Mules of Love*, 2002]

Could you say a little more about how your family's personal and historical legacy have shaped you as a person and a poet?

EB: My grandparents and parents, like many immigrant families, were not afraid of hard work. As I say that, I realize even that wording is theirs. They didn't expect things to come easily. But they did expect things to keep getting better. They had enormous optimism and they were willing to put their weight behind that. I appreciate their legacy of perseverance and hopefulness.

I'm somewhat of a pit bull. I don't give up easily. And I'm hopeful, sometimes to the point of foolishness. Of course I have learned by now that things don't just get better and better. And I'm sure that's not literally what they thought—I just absorbed it that way. So it was a hard landing to find out that I would make bad decisions, have bad luck, and suffer, just like most people.

I'm the only person in my family who has pursued a creative endeavor. My mother and father came from families with five children each and I am one of thirteen cousins on my mother's side and quite a few on my father's side as well. Among us all, there are no professional musicians, artists, dancers, singers, or writers, except me. So I'm somewhat of an anomaly.

However, my parents were both, in very different ways, devoted to precision. My father was a classic perfectionist. My mother, a devotee of doing everything with as much grace as possible. I've written in poems about the way she'd wrap a bottle of liquor from the store so the package looked like a modest work of art and she'd fold our clothes so beautifully they looked like they had just been taken off the shelf. There was nothing sloppy about my parents! And that's good training for a poet—precision, patience, perseverance.

AK: You write with great feeling and humor about domestic life, its banality and gritty consequence. One pictures you up to your hips in it much of the time (reminiscent in this and some other ways of the late, great Grace Paley).

Are there moments when glimmers of a poem occur to you just as you're doing an errand, or getting started in a squabble with your wife Janet or one of your kids, and you'd like to just stop everything and start capturing it in a poem . . . but you know it's not going to happen? Or are your domestically-rooted poems precipitates or distillates of situations that arise over and over, things that you can readily recollect in relative tranquility?

EB: What a high compliment to compare me—in any way at all—to Grace Paley. Thank you.

I welcome the times in ordinary, domestic life when a poem, as you say, begins to glimmer. Sometimes I take a few notes right then on whatever scrap of paper is handy. Other times I try to pay attention and remember as best as I can. Often the experiences are ones that have happened before, but suddenly I can see into them in a way that I couldn't before.

There was a pivotal moment in my marriage when I realized that every irritation was a possible poem. Every time I felt misunderstood or angry or sad, there was a poem there if I could only find it. And at that point I began to have a different relationship to discord. With the small annoyances, there was a happy excitement that I might have a poem. With more serious distress, there was at least an opportunity to explore more deeply.

AK: It might seem sexist to refer to your verse as "un-corseted," because one would not conventionally use the term to describe, for instance, Whitman's or Ginsberg's long-lined, sensuous, ecstatic, self-celebrating poems . . . although, come to think of it, in a gender-bending sort of way "un-corseted" could apply to their work, as well. Did reading Whitman or Ginsberg have any influence on your own development as a poet? How much of a struggle was it for you to arrive at that unapologetically open stance, or did it always come naturally to you?

EB: "Un-corseted" is another wonderful word! I imagine Whitman and Ginsberg would appreciate it too! And yes, they both were such deep influences. They opened up the poem, the line, as they opened their huge hearts. Each in his own way revolutionized poetry. I don't think any writer today could *not* have been influenced by them.

I was also influenced early on by Anne Sexton, who I was fortunate to study with at Boston University. While my other teachers were chipping away at my not-very-good poems, she encouraged me to expand, to write more, to stretch out. Her own groundbreaking work was thrilling and inspirational to me.

AK: I am not aware of other poets who, having staked out and intensely, lovingly expressed one sexual preference in their work, feel free to explicitly, wistfully yearn for what they've given up. Aside from the sexual politics of it all, you have insisted on your individual experience, and on complexity. What sorts of reactions, poetic and/or political, have you received for that? Has writing so honestly complicated your relations with your children?

EB: When any oppressed group is struggling for human rights, issues often need to be simplified to make progress. So, for example, in the fight for gay and lesbian rights we may say that being gay "isn't a choice." And that's true for many people, of course. However, it's not true for everyone. I have lived and made love with the same woman for 32 years, raised two children with her, and am more in love with her than ever. So I call myself a lesbian. But I'm not only a lesbian. I'm also someone who has had, before my marriage, passionate relationships with men. So, I'm bi-sexual by nature, but lesbian in practice. I think as the entirety of queer rights becomes more secure, people will understand that, like many things, sexual orientation can be complex.

That said, I adhere to Galway Kinnell's definition: "To me, poetry is somebody standing up, so to speak, and saying, with as little concealment as possible, what it is for him or her to be on earth at this moment." So I try to be transparent.

As for reactions, quite a few people have told me that they enjoyed that poem, "The Sad Truth." I think that even if they don't have the same experience as me, they have other experiences that have subtleties that aren't easily summed up into boxes. As for my children, they have been very generous and tolerant.

AK: Few contemporary poets work as consistently as you to connect the personal and the political, the local and the global. In some poems in *The Human Line* (Copper Canyon Press, 2007), you express fears for the planet in a very direct and intense way. Do you hope to mobilize an activist response, and have you had any experience of success with this if you do? Or is it really more of a *cri de coeur* over what we have been doing to the planet, and don't seem to be able to stop doing?

EB: Oh this is a very difficult question. It's hard for me to imagine that any poem of mine will have an impact on saving our planet. So I think they are, as you say, a *cri de coeur*.

And yet, although I don't have faith in *my* poems, I do have faith in Poetry. There are poems that have sustained me in the most painful times and taught me how to live. And I'll turn again to Orhan Pamuk here: "I believe literature to be the most valuable tool that humanity has found in its quest to understand itself. Societies, tribes, and peoples grow more intelligent, richer, and more advanced as they pay attention to the troubled words of their authors..."

So, although I don't think any of my poems are going to make a substantial contribution to saving our environment or even each other, I do think it's true that we can't make changes until we can conceive of those changes, until we can change the way we think. And poetry—and all literature—definitely help us do that. Like so much, it's a paradox. As Gandhi said, "Whatever you do will be insignificant, but it is very important that you do it."

AK: We are really looking forward to your reading. Looking at the list of our past readers, do you see the names of any poets who have been influences, teachers, friends?

EB: Oh yes! I first encountered many of these poets when Florence Howe and I were co-editing the first anthology of poetry by women, *No More Masks!* (Harper) in 1973! That title was taken from Muriel Rukeyser. She, along with Adrienne Rich, and many others here, were important early influences. Dorianne Laux was my mentor for many years and I am forever grateful to her for all she taught me. Billy Collins was extraordinarily kind, endorsing my first book in 2002 when I was trying to return to the world of poetry after a long hiatus. I'm privileged to teach with some of these poets, such as Marie Howe and

David St. John, and to call them friends. And Philip Levine recently discussed my poem, "What Did I Love," with Paul Muldoon on *The New Yorker*'s Poetry Podcast. I think that's the greatest honor of my poetry life.

• ● •

JILL BIALOSKY

• ● •

To borrow a metaphor from baseball, the setting and organizing metaphor for her poetry collection *The Players*, Jill Bialosky is a triple-threat: a major editor (at W. W. Norton), a well-reviewed three-time novelist, and an award-winning and accomplished poet. Bialosky is the author of four poetry collections: the aforementioned *The Players* (2014), *Intruder* (2008), *Subterranean* (2001), and *The End of Desire* (1997). But that still doesn't cover all of her bases: she's also an acclaimed memoirist and has co-edited an anthology, *Wanting A Child*. Her novels are *Under Snow*, *The Life Room* and, most recently, *The Prize*.

Bialosky's poetry has appeared in *The Paris Review*, *American Poetry Review*, *Kenyon Review*, *The New Yorker* and *The Atlantic*. She has been honored by The Poetry Society of America for her contributions to poetry. The *Los Angeles Times* praised *Intruder* in these terms: "Sharply perceptive, reminding readers about the way life forces us to our knees while restoring us to our true selves. In haunting imagery, the poems strike chords of recognition, like the way we hold on to moments, hoping to make them last forever even as we watch them dissolve."

KPS READING: NOVEMBER 2015

Andrew Kuhn: Hardly anyone is a full-time, nothing-but poet, but seemingly you more than most have other major occupations, any one of which, for a lot of people, would do nicely all by themselves. You're a top editor at Norton, and an increasingly prolific novelist and memoirist. Also a parent and wife. How do you decide when to pivot to poetry? Do you intentionally carve out time for it, or does poetry and the urge to make it take care of that for you, by insisting, even when it's inconvenient?

Jill Bialosky: Poetry is my first love, and I see myself first as a poet. Poetry made everything in my professional life possible. Through poetry I learned craft as a writer and I've taken those tools with me when I ventured into prose. I wrote an essay about it called "The Unreasoning Mask: The Shared Architecture of Poetry and Memoir," published on the *Kenyon Review* website. In that essay I argue that poetry and prose share a similar interior architecture. Not necessarily the structure, scaffolding, and formal issues of craft, though there can be similarities there as well, but thematic issues relating to intimacy of subject matter, tone, and connection with the reader. I pivot to poetry out of necessity. Between books I wait until the urgency presses itself forward and I have grown to rely on that method.

AK: Poetry has many different registers, and so does prose; in an era of colloquial diction in much of poetry these registers can overlap. Similarly, now that everyday life is fair game for both poetry and prose, there is no subject or venue that presents itself as presumptively poetic. How do you decide that an idea or an image or a situation is the kernel of a poem as opposed to the germ of a story or novel?

JB: That is an interesting and provocative question and I'm not sure I know how to answer it. When I wrote my memoir, *History of a Suicide: My Sister's Unfinished Life* (Washington Square Press, 2012), it was a book I thought about at least for a decade if not more, entered into, disengaged from over a long period of time, and then entered again. It was a book I wrote to try and understand an inexplicable event and it involved years of thinking about suicide, research, and personal investigation. I may continue that investigation in a piece of fiction. Voice calls itself to form and as a writer I allow that intuitive process to happen. Form, whether a poem, novel, or prose, is a vehicle for expression and artistic creation and ultimately it can't be forced.

AK: There's a poem in your collection *Intruder* (Alfred A. Knopf, 2010) which captures the tension and even at times the frank, jarring disjunction between an interior imaginative world and everyday contemporary life.

> Outside on the deck the poet read about ancient wars and vendettas,
> about a son protecting his mother from the dangers of her suitors.
> Inside the Knicks were on and she could hear the cheers
> and cursing through the screen.

The view veers with no warning between a poet's sensibility connected via the *Odyssey* to mythic situations and classic themes and a distant era, and shouts about the Knicks and video games. The poet's wish is stated plainly in the title, "Dreaming of Two Worlds Co-Existing in Harmony," but whether the dream can be realized remains seemingly unresolved.

> . . . . The long stems of the cosmos
> bent in the wind, and then a sound as primal as a first cry
> called over the mist, the screen door slammed shut,
> and across the field she saw the little one sneak away next door
> to fight another war on Nintendo.

The resolution seems comic, or mock-heroic. Is that about the best one can hope for these days, in bringing those two worlds into harmony?

JB: I like your reading of this poem. Again, I'm not quite sure I have an answer. That poem was a way to express the duality of the different layers of reality that exist within us, the outer world, the inner world, and the unconscious world and I believe that tension, for me, is the place in which art can crystalize. My sense is that the narrator in the poem recognizes that the wish, the dream of harmony isn't fully possible. She desires it and questions it. I don't want to close down the poem with interpretation. I want the reader to read his or her own experience into it.

AK: Other poems in *Intruder* are more ambiguous and surreal, and hew to a more consistently heroic rhetoric. "The Skiers," a cycle of ten unrhymed sonnets, for example, considers human figures and a mountain under various lights, evoking pitiless nature and human passion. The final poem reads in full:

> Across the peak the shadow of a deer
> and her hart neither frivolous nor star-
> struck and her slender, spotted, just-born fawn,
> legs still twisted from the womb, tucked behind
> and licked almost clean of its smell to pro-
> tect from harm as if to remind of the
> possibility of love. Once two bucks
> in agony fought to claim her scent. Un-
> furled by the ferocious wind, aroused, snow
> blows in circles, exposing what it meant
> to conceal. One version of paradise:
> Artemis, goddess of fertility
> and the hunt transformed into a stag. For
> one moment the world is perfectly calm.

The idea of Artemis herself transformed into a stag, and that being a version of paradise, is a pretty radical departure from the myths, I think; usually she's the one transforming others, preparatory to their being torn apart by hounds. Could you say a little about the imaginative and emotional origins of this cycle?

JB: It's been years since I wrote that poem and thought about it. At the time I was obsessed with the ideas in the poem, versions of paradise, as you say, desire and responsibility, fate. I set the poem on a mountain top because I had recently spent time skiing in the western mountains and was overwhelmed and awed by the natural world: its fierceness, intensity and threat. And I wanted the long poem to contain all that turmoil and beauty. It's meant to be allegorical in nature.

AK: In the collection *The Players* (Alfred A. Knopf, 2015), you begin with "Manhood," a cycle of thirteen plain-spoken yet mythically framed and paced poems built around our national pastime as experienced at the junior, family level. As a dad who still can't believe that the years of throwing batting practice are over, I can relate both to the sometimes intense parental investment you allude to and the fleeting poignancy of the whole project, which lends the cycle its elegiac tone.

> We sat in a group and drank our coffee
> and prayed that they'd get a hit.
> If they fumbled a ball or struck out
> we felt sour in the pit of our stomach.
> We paced. We couldn't sit still or talk.
> Throughout summer we watched
> the trees behind the field grow fuller
> and more vibrant and each fall
> slowly lose their foliage—
> it was as if we wanted to hold on
> to every and each leaf.

I gather that at this point your own son has long since grown out of his last uniform . . . . Does this cycle represent something of an ode or requiem for a phase in your and your family's life?

JB: I resist that interpretation. As in "The Skiers," the long sonnet sequence in *Intruder*, my method is to find a landscape in which to ground larger themes, ideas, and emotional and psychological realities. In the long sequence in *The Players* called "Manhood," I employed the baseball field as a canvas to ponder ideas of family and community, gender and coming of age. I chose the first person plural point of view to express ideas of shared identity and community. I see *The Players* as a book primarily about attachment and of course, it is elegiac as attachments take on different hues during the life cycle. The book, too, is about generations and certainly the emotional hue in the cycle achieves its register from the different voices it conjures.

AK: I take it, since you titled this cycle of poems "Manhood," that you set out not just to write about the "summer game" but to try to grasp what it might tell us about the mysterious essence of the male. There is a kind of fated stateliness to the succession of almost archetypal figures you embody in the poems, "Brothers," "The Fathers," "The Mothers," etc. Still and all, it's Little League (or Pony League, or Babe Ruth League, as later in the series the players are adolescents). Heart-breaking as it can be, baseball played by kids is also often hilarious when it's not mind-numbingly dull. Did it not strike you that way, a certain amount of the time? If so, did it seem that those aspects of the Little League experience were incompatible with the theme and tone you were trying to develop?

JB: As a female I was interested in exploring the world of gender in the poem and in that sense I see the poem as somewhat subversive. The long poem conjures an imagined world and in that world of the poem the players are serious baseball players who committed themselves to the sport for years. At one point I see them as cadets in training. As an outsider, observing, I came to appreciate the skill involved in the game. I did not see it as "hilarious" as you say, or "mind-numbingly dull." To the contrary, I found it exhilarating to be a spectator to the performance, commitment, camaraderie and skill involved. There is brutality to the game and to the language on the field and as an observer I wanted to embody that language, put it out there, see the ways in which language exerts power for these young boys becoming men and for the girls and the mothers who are witness and how this experience shapes all the various parties. I suppose there is playful irony at work—yes—that's true.

AK: Certainly there is great follow-through on the theme of contending with change and loss in the rest of the volume. Emptying a house, and the memories it evokes; the bittersweet experience of teaching a son to drive; the anxiety that comes when your offspring grow big enough that they go off on their own, into harm's way, and you don't even know—can't know—what's happening. Has your own experience of becoming an empty-nester been particularly unsettling, or is it just that pain makes better poems?

JB: I suppose I would best categorize the tone of the book as elegiac. The emotional surge in the work comes out of the ways in which relationships shift over time. I see the book guided by the principals of time and memory and attachment. The poems were written over a five-year period when I was very much in the thralls of the day to day world of motherhood. I don't believe in the notion that pain makes better poems. As a poet, I am committed to finding forms for expression and inquiry and beauty.

AK: We're very much looking forward to your reading. Looking at the list of our past readers, are there any who stand out as having been particularly influential in your own development?

JB: I'm honored to be a part of the distinguished series. Thank you for having me. Of the poets, several I studied with in graduate school, David St. John, Carol Muske-Dukes and Gerald Stern. I had the great privilege of working with Adrienne Rich as her editor over many of her later works, and too with Marie Howe, Donna Masini, Mark Doty and Li-Young Lee. Singling out the poets whose work has had an impact on my own would be almost like having to choose your favorite son. Poetry is a community of voices and I've admired and appreciated the work of many.

• ● •

GEORGE BILGERE

• • •

George Bilgere writes plainspoken poems about unpretentious people. His work packs a lyrical and emotional punch, a one-two that gets past your defenses and can knock you sideways. His six collections of poetry include *Imperial* (2014); Autumn House Poetry Prize winner *The White Museum* (2010); *Haywire* (2006), which garnered the May Swenson Poetry Award; and *The Good Kiss* (2002), selected by Billy Collins for the University of Akron Poetry Award. Other awards and grants include: the Midland Authors Award, a Pushcart Prize, and both Fulbright and National Endowment for the Arts grants. He has read at the Library of Congress and the 92nd Street Y.

To his enduring delight, Mr. Bilgere has appeared often on Garrison Keillor's "A Prairie Home Companion." Former U.S. Poet Laureate Ted Kooser chose six of Bilgere's poems for review and dissemination to newspapers around the country in his "American Life in Poetry" column, noting "neither of us [Kooser or Keillor] can get quite enough of this writer's clear, honest and moving work." Bilgere co-hosts his own delightful long-running weekly radio program, "Wordplay," which dares to put poems out over the air, and then invite discussion about them. He lives in Cleveland and teaches at John Carroll University.

KPS READING: MARCH 2015

Andrew Kuhn: First, this is a funny sort of housekeeping matter, but as a person who cares about how words sound, I hope you won't mind clarifying the correct way to pronounce your last name? And while you're at it, could you say a little about where the name came from, linguistically or geographically?

George Bilgere: The correct pronunciation of my last name has been a matter of conjecture in my family for generations. But I say "Bil-GARE," with a hard "g." We're originally from Austria, and came over with the other unwashed multitudes in 1850, eventually settling as farmers in Illinois and Missouri.

AK: Thanks for that. I can relate—my parents each pronounced our last name differently.
    You have spoken elsewhere about your decision to just go ahead and frankly make use of your life in your poetry, to dispense with masks or veils, to the extent that there doesn't seem to be a lot of daylight between your poetic persona and your personal presentation-of-self. Does that get tricky at family reunions, or when you start a new relationship? Although your tone is a lot cooler, do you feel any affinity for what used to be called the confessional poets?

GB: As a younger writer, I imitated the poets I most admired: Eliot, Yeats, and my mentor at Washington University, Howard Nemerov. It was all very lofty and sententious in terms of style, mostly because I didn't have much to write about *but* style. As I grew older and slowly came to have an actual life of my own I began to relax into my own particular idiom, my own voice. It was like finally finding a pair of shoes that fit. In my case, well-worn sneakers. And yes, I certainly did feel at one point for confessional poets like Lowell. In fact, I am much like Lowell, but without the immense talent. Both of us—and Yeats as well—relaxed in mid-career into a more conversational style.

AK: You grew up in post-war suburbia, like a lot of us, but unlike a lot of us you have written poems that capture both the golden promise and the bitter disappointment of that era. Judging strictly by events recounted in the poems, your family was initially comfortable, as your Dad's business selling cars thrived for a time. His alcoholism and your parents' divorce wrecked all that, and your family went through some not only emotional but literal hard times.

That leaves a mark, which shows up in the work in sometimes unexpected ways. In one poem, you internally address a pimply kid slaving away doing the grottiest jobs in a restaurant. The poem "Bus Boy" starts with a mock-elegiac rhetoric that contrasts with the setting, and what seems to promise to be an I've-been-there-pal kind of stance, which is comfortable for the reader, who may expect the poet will conclude with something conventionally encouraging, however ironic. But at the very end there's a big swerve:

> Like you, I was of the slime of alleys,
> of the same immemorial cigarette butts
> and rotting cottage cheese.
> And like you,
>
> I dreamed of a certain waitress,
> and of driving a fork into the forehead
> of the night manager,
> and of spitting in the soup
> of plump, complacent, well-dressed diners
> who snapped their fingers at me.
>
> But most of all I dreamed of being clean,
> and cool, and never, ever again
> slogging through the world's filth and stink,
>
> which is something I have achieved,
> as must be perfectly obvious to you.
>
> [From *Imperial*, 2014]

In the last line you emphatically distance your new self from this struggling loser in an in-your-face way that reads as harsh, and maybe anxious. It's not an unmixed pleasure for the poet to see how far he's come from having to do those nasty jobs—it seems he's got to remind himself, and the reader, of that fact, even though he's casually dressed, he's spotlessly clean, sporting a smashing woman on his arm, and out of "the world's filth and stink" forever. It reads raw, neither emotionally nor politically correct. Is that the effect you intended? Does an early experience of loss sharpen your appreciation for and pride in everything you've won back for yourself?

GB: As for the lack of political correctness that emerges in the work that looks back on my family's often tumultuous past—in poems like "Bus Boy"—that kind of startling ending has become a characteristic trope, a favorite toy in the Bilgere bag of tricks. Billy Collins says somewhere that he likes poems that are up to some mischief, and I like ambushing the reader's expectation that a lyric poem today is almost required to provide a little shot of good cheer and comfort in the form of an uplifting insight at the end. I take pleasure in turning that particular apple cart upside down from time to time.

AK: You have been a professor at John Carroll University in Cleveland for a good while, and you have a couple of poems that take a wry if not jaundiced view of the academic life. In one, the news that the poet has been granted tenure is anti-climactic, to say the least; in another, the prospect of wading through another stack of essays about ambiguity in Robert Frost seems distinctly less appealing that doubling down on the table wine. Do you find it's a challenge, keeping your own appreciation of the canon fresh while teaching undergraduates?

GB: Keeping things fresh in the face of the unrelenting onslaught of undergraduates—yes, it can be tough. Elvis Presley was once asked by a nervous young reporter after a concert whether he thought his performance had gone well. "Well darlin'," said the King, peering over his shades. "There's only so many times you can sing 'Heartbreak Hotel' and really give a fuck."

But the great thing about teaching literature is that there's always a new way to approach a writer. Just because "Stopping by Woods on a Snowy Evening" is a great poem doesn't mean you have to teach it every year. So many great Frost poems, so little time.

AK: I should say that there is evidence that you have more fun at John Carroll than readers of your poetry alone might suspect. I came across podcasts of "Wordplay," the radio show you have been doing for something like a decade with the poet John Donoghue. I am guessing it may be the longest-running poetry show on radio, in the U.S. at least, and it's very good listening. You guys are obviously fond of each other, riff together well, but also weave poetry into the conversation in a natural way that illuminates the work without pedantry. Everything else aside, it makes the listener want to take a poetry course with you . . . On one I listened to, you even read an accomplished, ambitious poem by one of your students, and joked about publishing it under your own name.

How did you get started doing a poetry show on the radio? Is there a way that radio and poetry go together particularly well?

GB: How "Wordplay" got started was quite simple. Many years ago I read that terrific Dana Gioia essay in *The Atlantic*, "Can Poetry Matter?"

The essay ends with a list of things poetry lovers can do to bring poetry to a wider audience, an audience beyond the ivory tower. And one suggestion Gioia gives is to start a poetry radio show.

Brilliant, I thought. And I took him at his word. I'm really proud of the show, which has developed a large and devoted listenership in Cleveland. And I must say its success is largely due to my co-host, John Donoghue, who is quite simply the best reader of poetry I've ever heard.

AK: You've been something of a favorite of Garrison Keillor, with your work featured on "A Prairie Home Companion" and "Writer's Almanac" numerous times. Do you think that doing your own radio show has made your poetry more radio-friendly over the years, or did it work the other way around? Do you know if Keillor is a listener of yours?

GB: Garrison Keillor has been such a generous and wonderful supporter of my work over the years. He's read my stuff on "Writer's Almanac" like fifty times. And one of the highlights of my career—no, my life— has been appearing as a guest on "A Prairie Home Companion."

And yes, certainly listening to his show and doing my own little program has influenced my sense that the poems I most like are the ones that are "radio ready," that offer enough in a first hearing to beguile, rather than baffle. I'm not sure if Garrison has heard "Word- play." But I'd like him to know that if he's interested in being a guest on the show I'd be willing to give him a chance. It could make all the difference to his career.

AK: Mr. Keillor, you heard it here first.

Your poems tend to hew to a quasi-conversational diction that can lull the reader into a certain kind of comfort that approaches complacency. We think we know where we are, we think we know what kind of a person we're hearing out, we may even think we know what's coming. Often, though, the place in other poems that merits the bland descriptor of "the turn" could be better described in yours as "the sucker punch." One example of this is quoted here in full.

Treptower Park, Berlin

We bicycled somberly around the great monument,
our somberness adjusted to about seventy thousand.
The other visitors to the monument that morning
were somber to more or less the same degree,
which was not coincidental, as all of us had passed
before the same bronze plaque at the entrance
explaining about the seventy thousand, the bombings,
the ratio of soldiers to civilians, Russians to Germans,
in a couple of long, complicated paragraphs
full of treaties, pacts, provisos, and Roman numerals.

It was a lovely day for being somber,
for trying somehow to feel the beautiful ghostly weight
of seventy thousand, although actually I think
it would have felt roughly the same if it were forty thousand,
or even ten. In truth, there aren't that many levels

of somberness available. There's basically just this hushed,
solemn way of moving around a monument,
staring at the obelisks, the big heroic statues,
the alphabetical plaques of names, as we smile
at the foreigners who smile right back,
everyone a bit anxious, eager to please, like,
Hey, no way this could ever happen again. Right?

[From *Imperial*, 2014]

To borrow an old-fashioned expression from my mom, this is a nervy poem. Conjuring ironically with mass death in WWII is a high-wire move to begin with, even though this particular setting is about a memorial for Russian soldiers killed in the Battle of Berlin, and not the holocaust as such. The mild oxymoron of "bicycled somberly" sets the tone, and the deadpan aside about the seventy-thousand level of somberness, versus the forty- or even ten-thousand, raises the stakes. But the bemused, distancing stance collapses in the final line, the final word. "Right?"

Have you caught any flak for this poem, so to speak? Is it trickier now to deal with large, public, historical events in poetry than it was at other points in history?

GB: You asked about the risk in poems like "Treptower Park." Yes, I've caught flak from that poem—and others that fail to behave properly. Again, as with "Bus Boy," I resist the notion that there is an "official" way to approach a cow, however sacred it may be. My own approach to the world—being, after all, a Boomer—consists of many, many laminated layers of protective ironic detachment. Layers with names like Nixon, Watergate, Vietnam, Iraq, Cheney. Not to somehow include this complex layering would seem dishonest.

AK: Maybe because you address the reader in such an engaging way— and the argument of each poem is absorbing, and the associative leaps startling—on the first reading one can miss how much beautiful language is happening. The poem quoted here in full provides one example:

Magellan

When a beautiful woman lies down
On her brown belly, on her pink beach towel,
And reaches back and behind to perform
That curious legerdemain whereby
Her dazzling white
Bikini top is undone
And she stretches out under the sun,

I continue watching the breakers
Stagger to their knees, and listen
To the gulls work through
Their chronic desolation,
Thinking, for some reason,
Of my mother, struggling
Into the cross-stitched straitjacket
Of her girdle
Before a night out with my father,
And I think of the boundless
Surge and heave of the oceans,
Swollen and unfettered
Before any man, crazed
By indifferent beauty, raised
White sails to cup
The wind's breasts
And girdle the globe.

[From *The Good Kiss*, 2002]

The breakers staggering to their knees, the chronic desolation of the gulls, the cross-stitched straitjacket of the girdle, the white sails cupping the wind's breasts—on any one of these a poem could have been founded. You scatter them almost casually, and the reader gathers them up, delighted but unsurprised, because these are the sorts of things we've learned to expect to find, strolling this particular beach.

When you started writing "Magellan," did you know where you were going, or did you too start out in the emotional state of the man "crazed by indifferent beauty," compelled to follow where it led? Were you surprised where you ended up?

GB: Thanks for those kind words about "Magellan!" It's easy to forget, in a conversation about ideas and influences and technique, that what it really comes down to is language. My love of the English language, what John Updike called "this lovely fossil we carry around in our mouths," is what got me started in this whole mess in the first place. Writing poetry, reading and talking about poetry, has given me the best life I can imagine. And I can't wait to continue the conversation in Katonah.

• ● •

HOW A POEM CAN HAPPEN

DANIEL BROWN

• ● •

Daniel Brown, or Dan Brown, not to be confused with the author of Vatican conspiracy blockbusters, won the 2008 New Criterion Poetry Prize for his collection *Taking the Occasion*. Mr. Brown has an advanced degree in musicology, has taught music history and theory at Cornell and Dartmouth, and has published *Why Bach?*, an appreciation of the composer. His poems have appeared in *The New Criterion*, *Poetry*, *Parnassus*, and *Partisan Review*, and been anthologized in *Poetry 180*, *The Pushcart Prize*, and *The Swallow Anthology of New American Poetry*.

X.J. Kennedy called Brown's poems "splendid demonstrations of the power to be obtained by drawing the reins really tight." Of his second collection, *What More?* (2015), Clive James observed, "This poet, while less copious than many of his generation, gets much further because he can keep thinking while he laughs, and vice versa. I recommend *What More?* with a whole heart as one of the few modern books of poetry that has twice as much in it every time you read it, instead of half."

KPS READING: SEPTEMBER 2015

Andrew Kuhn: You've studied music seriously and lectured on it at the college level. Some of your poems vividly evoke aspects of the experience of listening to music. This is from "What More?"

> I couldn't have been as old as eight when my
> Response to music had broadened out enough
> To accommodate, along with all the love,
> A thought that could be taken to imply
>
> Some criticism: that music certainly
> Did plenty of repeating, didn't it. . . .
>
> Why shouldn't notes be streaming ever on
> To shapes and traceries forever new:
> A state late Debussy was drifting to,
> A dream an avant-garde was bent upon . . . .
>
> Of course one asking this would be forgiven
> If his voice were short a certain urgency,
> His having been conveyed repeatedly
> By music to the cumulus of heaven.

[From *What More?* 2001]

Could you say a little about if, or in what ways, your knowledge of and appreciation for music have informed your involvement with poetry?

Daniel Brown: It may seem odd, what with all the talk about the "music" of poetry, but I don't see either my reading or writing of poems as having much to do with music. Maybe that's because I've spent enough time with each of these arts to have a marked sense of their dissimilarities. Poetic rhythm seems very different to me from musical rhythm: a comedian's timing is closer to it than a composer's. (Though a Victor Borge can combine the two.)

As for the other main "musical" aspect of poetry—euphony (as embodied in assonance, alliteration, rhyme)...what Yeats called the articulation of sweet sounds together—I can't think of a real cognate for it in music. If music has influenced my poetry, it's been by showing that an artwork can at least *seem* "perfect:" not a note wasted, every element contributing to the effect....

AK: No doubt you've noticed that not everybody who writes poetry rhymes these days, in fact there are people who vociferously disapprove of the practice. Some poets will rhyme in some poems—one may almost have the impression that they do it just to prove they can—but don't in most of their work.

You on the other hand rhyme far more often than not. Certainly not always in patterns that are conventional or readily apparent, and sometimes in a "slant" way that might even be overlooked (or rather go unheard) on first reading—but it's there. What is your relationship with rhyme, if I may put it like that, and why do you think so many current poets eschew rhyme?

DB: I'm shocked to hear that not everybody rhymes, but if you say so.... It's easier for me to say where my relationship with rhyme came from than to say what it is. The first poet I fell for in a big way was Frost. Many of his poems rhymed, and in emulation of them I started rhyming too—and have never seen a reason to stop. The aural appeal of rhyme is a powerful weapon in a poet's arsenal, and while there's certainly no *need* to wield it—and I love tons of free verse poems— I've yet to hear a non-fatuous argument for laying that weapon down altogether.

And it's not like rhyme can't be fresh: Frost himself showed this in his play of common speech rhythms across the meter. (Rappers do something similar.) There's also something miraculous about the improbability, the against-all-oddsness, of rhyme. And if you can perform a miracle, how can you not indulge that capability, at least occasionally?

AK: There's an interesting tension or at least a seeming contrast in your poems between the structure—again, the use of rhyme—and the authorial voice, which tends to be colloquial, chatty, unpretentious. One surprising effect you often manage is to seem unhurried, even expansive, in a relatively short poem. You're not grabbing the reader by the lapels so much as striking up a conversation with a willing stranger. Were you always that confident that you could capture the reader's attention in a low-key way?

DB: I've always *wanted* to do that (whether I was confident I could is another matter, but it would seem, at a minimum, that I wasn't ruling out the possibility). My poems often say things I can imagine myself really saying to someone (that someone being precisely, in your apt and insightful phrase, "a willing stranger"). So as I'm writing, I tend to hear myself literally (as distinguished from literarily) speaking to a listener. If you're hearing that too, then one of my main hopes for my stuff is being realized.

AK: There was a time when "light verse" was a perfectly respectable thing to aspire to do well, and the masters of it—Ogden Nash springs to mind—were not only widely beloved but esteemed. Some of your work seems to harken back to this tradition. Here is one example, quoted in full:

> **Men**
>
> Haven't they the least resistance?
> Let a looker amble by
> And watch the heads turn helplessly.
> Talk about action at a distance!
> It's not like Newton, fruit unfallen,
> Wouldn't have had a thing to go on.
>
> [From *What More?*, 2015]

Do you see yourself as, among other things, a practitioner of light verse? What does it say about the culture that readers and writers have to such a great extent lost the knack for it?

DB: I do see some of my poems as funny, but not only so—which is why I myself wouldn't call them "light." I'd like to think even the (hopefully) funny ones speak to some significant human truth (as the one you cite self-evidently does, it seems to me). As to why "purely" light verse—verse that "just" wants to be funny—has fallen out of favor, I haven't got a clue, especially since when people do read it they seem to enjoy it as much as ever.

It's also possible to overstate light verse's unpopularity. Isn't Shel Silverstein one of the country's best-selling poets? Billy Collins certainly is—though whether even his funniest poems could be called "light" is an open question. (My own view is that they shouldn't be, and I wouldn't be surprised if he agreed.)

AK: Another quality of your poems which is unusual these days, but didn't used to be, is that they tend to articulate an argument. In this, as in their frank lustiness and structured rhyming, they're reminiscent (to me anyway) of the ironically named metaphysical poets of the seventeenth century. Like theirs, your poems are *about* something—often, they make a case—that for didactic purposes, for instance, could be paraphrased, albeit at greater length and less gracefully. One sharp example is your wry, back-handed appreciation of "Young Avis"—who "consecrates his future to . . . / To one involving nothing new." Here are the last two stanzas.

> Of course an urge to innovate
> Is less than an *essential* trait.
> Nor need the soul be horrorstruck
> If someone wants to chase a buck.
>
> Besides, a guy disposed to know
> How high it's in himself to go
> (And better than to aim for higher)
> A soul could practically admire.

[From *What More?* 2015]

Is there anything in the way of defiance in your being as frankly old-fashioned as this? Or is it just how things occur to you, the diction and the form that best suits what you mean to say?

DB: I confess to a preference for subjects (and find it unfortunate that in the current climate a confession is called for). I see this preference not as defiant but as salutary. Subjects can be a tremendous power source for poems, and tapping into a subject's power is among the most absorbing and rewarding tasks a poet can take on. (These thoughts are expressed more fully in "A Brief Brief for Subjects," a series of posts I contributed to the *Best American Poetry* blog.)

I do see some affinity in my work with "metaphysical" practices (and George Herbert is one of my very favorite poets), but I don't think of my work as old-fashioned. Maybe I'm fooling myself, but for all its formality I hear a new note in it: a New York voice. In the Avis poem, the last stanza (especially its last line) has more of the East River in it than the Thames.

AK: I don't know if she's been an influence on you or not, but your poetry in its rhyme and rhythm and wit and willingness to make accessible assertions reminds me of Kay Ryan, who read for us not long ago. Looking at the list of past readers for the Series, do you see any who have influenced you in any way?

DB: I'm flattered that you see similarities, which I acknowledge, between Kay Ryan's work and mine, but I think there are some considerable differences too, and I don't see her as an influence. Now that I've looked at it, the Katonah list as an astonishing whole has influenced me— if inducing awe counts as influence—but as far as particular poets, it would seem that even the matchless prestige of your series hasn't brought Frost or Dickinson to your dais (not yet, anyway).

• ● •

BILLY COLLINS

• • •

Billy Collins needs no introduction, but will get one here anyway. He served two terms as U.S. Poet Laureate (2001–2003) and served as New York State Poet Laureate from 2004 to 2006, while continuing to steer the Katonah Poetry Series and write marvelous, beloved poems. His more recent collections include *The Rain in Portugal* (2016); *Aimless Love: New and Selected Poems* (2013), *Horoscopes for the Dead: Poems* (Random House, 2012), and *Ballistics: Poems* (2008). He's been awarded well over a dozen prestigious awards in poetry, most recently the Peggy V. Helmerich Distinguished Author Award (2016).

A gifted and dedicated teacher, Collins has served on the faculty of Lehman College, Sarah Lawrence, SUNY Stony Brook Southampton, and the Winter Park Institute. His two *Poetry 180* anthologies, developed during his laureate tenure and widely used in schools, have helped ignite a passion for poetry in an entire generation. He has enormously widened the audience for spoken poetry via Garrison Keillor's radio program "A Prairie Home Companion," popular CD recordings, and live readings all over the country (including three at the White House). As a poet, anthologist, reader, and sly polemicist—in each of these roles showing unparalleled reach—Billy Collins has done more to bring poetry back towards the center of American culture and conversation than anyone since Robert Frost.

KPS READING: APRIL 2014

Andrew Kuhn: You have been involved with the Katonah Poetry Series for a long time, happily for all of us. Can you say a little about how that came to be, and how the series and your engagement with it have changed over the years?

Billy Collins: My then wife and I moved into an old mid-nineteenth century house in northern Westchester in 1989. We had been living in Scarsdale, and like many people in that part of the county, we never ventured to the north. So the scene was very new to us. Then one day I found in a local paper that William Matthews was going to be reading at the Katonah library the following Sunday. That's how I discovered the series, then run by its founder, Robert Phillips.

I was amazed that some of the top poets in the country would be coming to my local library. When Phillips accepted a job offer from the University of Houston, he left a career in advertising and asked me if I would take over as director. A natural born shirker of official responsibilities, I hesitated. But in the end I promised to bring the series into its twenty-fifth year—in two years' time—but I ended up at the helm for, I think, fifteen years. Now the reins are in the capable hands of others who are kind enough to consult me on their choice of poets.

AK: Your poems accommodate readers in ways that readers of poetry have learned they cannot take for granted with other poets. You tell us where we are, in time, space, weather; you describe things in such a way that we can readily picture them; you respect conventions of grammar and punctuation; you tend not to use jargon or vocabulary that would require most of us to fire up the browser (unless you're kidding, which does happen).

Beyond that, you have spoken about the poem as a sort of conversation with the reader, and the conversational tone you take is another way you engage us. At this point, it is what we expect in a Billy Collins poem. But did you always write this way? If not, how did your poetic values and voice evolve?

BC: Well, you just pretty much described the style of a Billy Collins poem, if we can say there is such a thing. But those features did not become visible until later in my writing when I came under a helpful set of influences. It seems we are all born with about two hundred bad poems in us. Some people have the good sense to die with them intact and unexpressed. Others, who want to write, have to exorcise the bad ones, and the only way to do that is write them out.

Early on, I thought poetry had to be mysterious, so I wrote mysteriously. Now I feel that a good poem is a mix of the clear and the mysterious. It's crucial to grasp the difference. I would say most bad poems either are mysterious about something that should be clear (like you're on a sailboat) or clear about something that will always remain mysterious (like the soul).

AK: Your commitment to readability, and your hostility to obscurantism, has earned you some critical brickbats from people who seem to mistake simplicity of address, for instance, for simple-mindedness. Despite the mild and bemused persona in most of your poems, you've given at least as good as you've got, both in interviews (*The Paris Review* one springs to mind) and in poetry. The title poem of *Ballistics* (Random House, 2004) concludes with a fantasy about shooting up a recent volume by "someone of whom I was not fond." In it, you mention "the poems about his childhood // and the ones about the dreary state of the world."

Was it always a bad idea to build a poem around these topics, or has it become a worse idea recently? If so, why is that?

BC: In that poem I wanted "poems about his childhood" to represent narrowly autobiographical poetry and "ones about the dreary state of the world" to represent broadly and explicitly political poetry, both of which have imaginative limits. As for the critical opinion that my poems are too simple, my response is: go "problematize" them. After all, that's what keeps a lot of critics busy these days.

AK: You are, it's safe to say, the most famous and successful poet in America today, if not of all time. Yet you didn't publish your first collection until you were forty. Were you passionately devoted to poetry from early on, or did it creep up on you?

BC: Like Kay Ryan I was afraid to be that embarrassing thing known as a poet, yet at the same time, I wanted nothing more than to be one. An odd bind. I was writing all along, beginning in high school right through graduate school (Ph.D. in English, of all things) and into my teaching career. Frankly, it just took me a long time to figure out a way of writing that made me happy. I later learned that these poems made other people happy too. Who would have guessed?

AK: Is it weird to be both a poet and a celebrity? Rock musicians end up writing a lot of songs about being rock musicians; writers like Norman Mailer who became celebrated early end up wrestling, sometimes interestingly and sometimes not, with issues of fame. Poets in the last fifty years haven't had to deal with this much. Do you find that the fact of your fame creates any extra static or complication, any sense that you have to intentionally set it aside when you sit down with yourself to write?

BC: It's just time consuming, like managing a little business. Seamus Heaney said that you have to learn "how to survive your success." It drags you from the private place where you write (think of how children like hiding places) into the world. I like Bob Fosse's take on success: "You spend half of your life struggling to be famous, and the other half hiding in a closet." Then there's Yeats calling himself "A sixty-year-old smiling public man." Sorry if I'm hiding behind a fence of quotations.

AK: You have spoken of your poetic persona or avatar as that of the *flaneur*, which is an evocative French term. My friends at Wikipiedia tell us this about the *flaneur*:

> Flaneur (from the French noun *flâneur*), means "stroller," "lounger," "saunterer," or "loafer." *Flânerie* refers to the act of strolling, with all of its accompanying associations. The *flâneur* was, first of all, a literary type from nineteenth-

century France essential to any picture of the streets of Paris. It carried a set of rich associations: the man of leisure, the idler, the urban explorer, the connoisseur of the street.

Were you a flaneur before you ever heard of the term, or were you won over to this stance after having read about it? Do you have any literary heroes who were or are flaneurs?

BC: Before my acquaintance with flaneuring (not a word, by the way) I was attracted to that figure in English Romantic poetry who wanders through the countryside—unlike the urban flaneur—often falling into a reverie, then writing a poem that is a mix of landscape and thought. He's a stroller, a dawdler, head in the clouds. My persona is really a modernized version of that character drawn primarily from Wordsworth and Coleridge. He is by nature a daydreamer whose favorite toys are his thoughts. Not content to leave the natural world alone, he uses its scenes as launching pads for imaginative flights. By the way, the flaneur tradition was recently revived in a terrific book by Teju Cole titled *Open City*.

AK: Some of your work does involve strolls through European land-scapes and cityscapes, but many more of your poems start in a room and, in narrative terms, stay there. The narrator shares with the flaneur an intentional lack of intention, but there's a subtle tension there at the outset, which I have come to experience as the question, *How is he going to get out of it this time?*

There's a Houdini-like aspect to your poems, which so often start in a state of confinement (more comfortable, certainly, than locked up in a chest), or a determinedly banal situation (walking the dog, eating in a restaurant) and progress to an escape, however momentary, or imaginative, or rhetorical. Often humor provides a leg up, and the whole exercise feels like a bit of a lark. But even then there is a sense of something significant at stake, which often turns out to be, in some form or fashion, dealing with death. What is it about poetry that so many of its paths lead to "the Big D," as it is never, ever called? And how have you come to deal with it in these particular ways?

BC: I am beginning to wish my responses were as articulate and insightful as your questions! I find that starting with something mundane manages to include the reader and put pressure on me to find a way out of the mundane. You don't want to board a plane in Miami then land in Miami a few hours—or lines—later. So the poem has to "escape" its initial confinement. There are lots of doors leading into bigger rooms, but the two big ones for poets are clearly marked "LOVE" and "DEATH." The shadow of mortality falls across the page and would darken it completely if the possibility of love were not available.

AK: There's a kind of abstemiousness or austerity about the poetic limits you have set for yourself. You decline to make many of the usual claims poets often try to make on a reader's attention: a tone of high moral seriousness; grisly or shocking narrative material; displays of dazzling technique with difficult forms (except, again, when you're joking around); elaborate sonic or rhythmic effects; extremes of emotional intensity. You also refrain from making large claims on the readers' time. Stanzas are mostly short—three lines, typically—and your longest poems don't run much more than about forty lines.

Do you have lockers full of notebooks with rhymed fantasy epic poems teeming with characters, or sonnet cycles about your childhood, or multi-part allusive cantos referring to obscure historical events in a variety of languages? Any deconstructive tone poems in there?

But seriously, do you ever get a yen to try something completely different? Do you think you might catch a lot of grief if you did, like Dylan going electric at the Newport Folk Festival?

BC: No secret lockers. What you see is what you get. And I'm not really interested in developing because I still find in my persona an agreeable voice and a lasting source of curiosity. He still has a lot to explore. If I could only think of it! If a poet is lucky and smart enough to create a lasting persona, a kind of vocal character, then he or she can ride that persona into the grave. Writing poetry for me is not like trying on different costumes. A lot of that went on before I knew what I was doing. See aforementioned late bloomer.

AK: Poetry was originally a spoken art, and you have delivered more poetry, aloud, in your own voice, than anyone around. Your appearances on "A Prairie Home Companion" had over four million listeners; recently on "The Colbert Report" over a million people heard you and Stephen Colbert read alternating stanzas. But you also have a heavy schedule of live readings all over the country. Is there something about hearing poetry aloud, particularly as read by the poet, for which there is really no substitute?

BC: Well, in some cases, the listener wishes there *were* a substitute! Not every poet knows how to make friends with the microphone or the audience. When I compose a poem, I never read it aloud to myself or the cat. But I know exactly how it will sound when I read it for the first time from a stage because I hear every syllable as I am writing. I hear it in silence. I write with the ear. Much of my fiddling with a poem after its initial run is aimed at making the poem sound better.

AK: Looking back at the list of the poets who have read for the series, can you name a few whose work had an influence on your own, or with whom you had a particularly good time when they came to town?

BC: It's a truly impressive list of poets, and because influences wash over one from all sides, it's hard to isolate a few.

But I learned from Katha Pollitt how clear, simple diction can keep emotion under control. Immense debts to James Tate and the late Paul Violi for their larky humor, and to William Matthews for showing me how you include in poems your taste and your learning. Violi, it should be said, was one of the most faithful attendees of the Katonah Poetry Series before his untimely death.

AK: We are very much looking forward to your reading, and appreciate enormously how much you've done and continue to do for the series.

• ● •

JIM DANIELS

• ● •

Jim Daniels, like Phillip Levine, came up in and around the auto industry in Detroit. His first three books—*Places/Everyone* (1985), *Punching Out* (1990), and *M-80* (1993)—draw heavily on the auto factory experience. He has branched out, thematically and geographically, in his later volumes, but cars are still imaginatively important: the title of his Blue Lynx poetry prize winning collection is *Revolt of the Crash-Test Dummies* (2007). Jim Daniels is for sure the only American poet with one of his poems emblazoned on the roof of a bona fide racecar (poem: "Factory Love;" driver: Alexander Grabau; car: white Mitsubishi Evolution II CE9A).

Mr. Daniels is prolific, with fifteen collections published to date. More recent titles include *Birth Marks* (2013), *All of the Above* (2011), and *Having a Little Talk with Capital P Poetry* (2011). Daniels has also won many teaching awards at Carnegie Mellon, where he has been a professor since the 1980s. His poetry has won awards from the National Endowment for the Arts and The Pennsylvania Council on the Arts. He won the Brittingham Prize for Poetry and the Tillie Olsen Prize from the Working-Class Studies Association for *Street*, a book of poems paired with photographs by Charlee Brodsky. He has edited or co-edited numerous significant anthologies, including *Letters to America: Contemporary American Poetry on Race* (1995).

KPS READING: OCTOBER 2014

Andrew Kuhn: You have traveled further from where you came from to where you are than a lot of people your age, certainly than most poets and professors. Can you say a little about that journey, and some of the different ways it has informed your work over the years?

Jim Daniels: Despite the fact that I've taught writing for over thirty years now, where I come from—a white, working-class neighborhood on the edge of Detroit—continues to inform my writing. It's where I'm from literally and emotionally; it's where I went through childhood and emerged on the other side, so it's a rich source of material for me. Also, many of the people I am closest to still live there, so I am still connected emotionally to the place and return there often (I was just there four days ago). It informs my work in that I continue to write about work of all kinds (the "Tenured Guy" poems in *Having a Little Talk With Capital P Poetry* [Carnegie Mellon, 2011], for example).

AK: You have written in stark and unlovely terms about working and working class life; it's not exactly PC (politically correct, that is). There's not a lot of feel-good solidarity in the "Digger" poems, for example, when the narrator is being socialized into intentionally busting the assembly line so everybody gets a breather. Kind of makes the reader think about the decline and fall of industrial America in slightly less tragic terms. Did you think about a political text or subtext in these poems when you wrote them? Have you had any surprising responses to this work from a political angle? Do you consider yourself a political person, or a political poet?

JD: As soon as you start writing with a political agenda, you're limiting yourself. Life, and poetry, are more complicated than that. The stereotypes emerge and the writing reads like propaganda. I feel that my work is political simply through my choice of subject matter. Examining these lives in my writing says they are important and should be a part of our literature. A lot of the struggles of those lives involve asserting your individuality in the face of forces designed to make you more anonymous, so workplace sabotage was just one of the ways of asserting that individuality. I also believe that the literature of work is crucial to our understanding of our lives—not just working-class jobs, but all jobs.

AK: In terms of non-PC poetry, though, a strong case could be made that your powerful long poem "Time, Temperature" (*Blessing the House*, 1997) about race and race conflict over decades in Detroit represents an absolute high water mark (alright, possibly excepting Bukowski). You give the "N" word such a workout that it retains or recovers its percussive, nasty power, even after what is now decades of habituation and numbing caused by its routine appearance in rap lyrics. Part of the shock, of course, is that it's a white man using it, and not casually but angrily, with anguish, even despairingly. Can you talk about how that poem came to be, how it was received, and how you experience it now?

JD: PC poetry can be bland poetry that can come off as self-righteous or self-serving, when in poetry we need to examine our own lives honestly. "Time, Temperature" was the longest poem I ever wrote until "Niagara Falls," and the reason is that I had repressed writing about race for so long (see comment on Baldwin below) that when I opened that door, all this stuff came spilling out.

It was a hard poem to write and revise. I've only read the poem aloud a couple of times—once at an AWP (Associated Writing Programs) conference, and once in Detroit at Marygrove College. In Detroit, I got one of the few standing ovations I've received at a reading ever from a very diverse audience, and it nearly brought me to tears.

Obviously, racism continues to be a huge problem in this country, and many of the problems that Detroit continues to have are linked to racial issues, so while I think the poem reflects a particular time period, I believe it is still relevant.

AK: The poem is dedicated to James Baldwin. Can you say why? Was his writing a major influence on you? How do you think Baldwin would have responded to "Time, Temperature"?

JD: I had James Baldwin as a teacher for a course in graduate school at Bowling Green, and in that class, he challenged us to examine our own lives honestly in terms of race. At that time, I was not up to the challenge. I consider that poem like a late paper for his class.

Ernest Champion, an ethnic studies professor at Bowling Green had invited Baldwin as a visiting professor. When they opened the James Baldwin room at Bowling Green after his death, I sent a copy of the book to Champion to put in the room. I also edited an anthology, *Letters to America: Contemporary American Poetry on Race* (Wayne State University Press, 1995), as further work in this area, and at Carnegie Mellon, I started the Martin Luther King, Jr. Day Writing Awards for local students, which is in its sixteenth year. So I continue to be interested in having honest discussions about difference through poetry.

AK: Many of your poems are about as plainspoken as could be, almost defiantly non-figurative. As in some of Frost's earlier work there are long dramatic monologues that portray a character in a very specific place and time, but you go well beyond Frost in your commitment to keeping the language scrupulously colloquial and non-literary. Here is an example from Niagara Falls":

> I can afford this bad meal
> and our hotel room in Niagara Falls.
> Some people think I'm cheap,
> the way I can't relax
> about money, counting it,
> making sure. I envy the easy grace
> of credit card and keep the change.
> My parents never stayed in hotels
> or went out to eat.
> We stayed at home. At home, we ate.

[From *Show and Tell: New and Selected Poems*, 2003]

One of the striking things about this strategy is that it denies the speaker in the poem, and the reader, one of the consolations of poetry, which is the prospect and pleasure of the little escape that's accomplished when you use language to turn something into something else. In a lot of these poems, as in the lives they describe, "It is what it is" isn't a bland tautology, it's a grim fact not only of their lives but of their minds.

There's an austerity to the discipline you bring to this voice that's bracing, and certainly comes across as authentic. But it can also seem pretty relentlessly dour. Does life really suck that consistently in Warren, Michigan? For everybody? Or, putting it another way, do you think that this strategy fully honors the potential emotional and imaginative range even of the hard-up, beaten down, indifferently educated narrators of these poems?

JD: I am not overtly conscious when I write of using figurative language or not, but I know that I don't use as much as a lot of poets. I think it might have something to do with what I'm writing about. Using figurative language can perhaps seem like a luxury if you're in the middle of the assembly-line or having a gun pointed at you. There's a relentless urge to be understood, to be clear.

I'm not sure "honoring" is a word that I would be concerned with. Acknowledging, yes, but not so concerned with honoring anyone. I can't—and don't try to—speak for everyone in Warren or Detroit or working-class or whatever. Someone wrote to me after my book of stories, *Detroit Tales* (Michigan State University Press, 2003), was published, to complain that my stories didn't reflect their Detroit, and I said, of course not, we all have our own tales, and those are just mine.

Of course, I don't intend to be relentlessly dour. I have sort of a dark, fatalistic sense of humor, so sometimes I think something is funny, but no one else does. Same with range—people will react differently to my work in ways that I can't control. I can only hope it can find an audience out there somewhere in the poetry landscape.

AK: Which it certainly has . . . . Switching gears for a minute, how do you feel about Bruce Springsteen? You're of about the same generation, and conjure with a lot of the same materials, including what living through the rusting of the rust belt feels like, growing up confused in a tough and ugly place. But you don't give us the soaring sax and the screaming redemption—it's a lot darker at the edge of your town. Are you ever tempted to resolve to that major chord, or would that represent a feel-good cheat, a surrender to sentiment?

JD: I remember first seeing Springsteen at the Masonic Temple in Detroit in 1978. I saw Bob Seger at Pine Knob (an outdoor music facility on the outskirts of Detroit) the same week. That was a pretty exciting week, despite the hearing loss I may have experienced.

I write a lot of poems about music, and first connected to writing through music more than the poetry we were studying in school. I would like a sax player to accompany me at all my readings, or an electric guitar. Or back-up singers. Yes, definitely back-up singers.

I guess I'm not that conscious of how things resolve in terms of darkness and light, so I am not tempted usually to alter things to lighten them up. I do remember one poem from my first book, *Places/ Everyone* (University of Wisconsin Press, 1985), called "My Father Worked Late," where I'd tacked on an ending that was somewhat more hopeful, but an editor called me out on it, and she was right—the ending was a kind of wishful thinking—I was thinking more about my relationship with my father than I was the poem. So, I cut that ending and left it with:

> *Give, Give, I give.*
> As if there was anything left
> to give.

Which, I admit, is a pretty much of a downer.

AK: But—and—a very strong close to the poem . . . . Even closer to home than Springsteen, of course, there's Eminem, another native son of Warren. Addressing him in "Can't Sleep," your narrator notes, "Your mother could / have been any number of my classmates: / Lynn, Robin, Patty, Cindy M., Cindy R.," . . . . The poem is framed by a news snippet noting that the rapper had canceled a tour owing to a dependency on sleep medication. This did in fact occur in August 2005, when Eminem was 33, at which point he was still the number-one selling male artist in the world, though his figures were down from the 19 million copies that his Marshall Mathers LP had sold worldwide.

Does it feel strange, as a highly respected and successful poet with a record of achievement spanning decades, to have a punk kid zoom up behind you straight out of your backyard and become a multimillionaire household name spouting what, as poetry, reads as rageful doggerel? In one of your poems you mention Gil Scott-Heron, a jazz musician whose elegant and allusive spoken-word compositions prefigured rap, or hip-hop; prophetically, a group from that same era styled themselves "The Last Poets." Is there still a way for literary poetry and rap or hip-hop to connect and maybe enrich one another, or has that ship sailed, or long since been sunk in the harbor?

JD: Oh yeah, Marshall. He reminds me very clearly of certain guys I went to high school with—a different generation, obviously, but the same attitude and edge. A lot of punk kids in Warren. They filmed part of *Eight Mile* at a trailer park very close to where I grew up.

I don't resent him at all, just like I don't resent more successful poets—and there's a lot of them. This may sound hokey, but at this point in my career, I guess I don't really care, but I consider myself very, very lucky to have found poetry and been successful enough to have this great job at Carnegie Mellon University that rewards me for what I do and gives me time to continue to do it.

I clearly remember hearing Gil Scott-Heron on WABX, an "underground" radio station, when I was in high school and being excited by his work. I'd never heard anything like it. There's always an intersection where music and poetry merge—I'm not one to say this is poetry and that isn't poetry. I also remember seeing Public Enemy here in Pittsburgh shortly after *Do the Right Thing* came out. I was intrigued by their blend of words and music. In fact, I wrote a poem about going to that concert. Some young guys in the audience thought me and my friend Frank were undercover cops.

AK: You probably know that the Katonah Poetry Series has featured many distinguished poets over the years. Looking at the list of past readers, do you see poets who have influenced your own development?

JD: I love the list of previous readers for the range of voices there. I get a bit discouraged when I see poetry defined too narrowly to the exclusion of a lot of important voices. Of course, Phil Levine is important to me. The weird thing is that I came to him late—I was already in grad school before I read any of his work. Phil has been an inspiration on many levels and I am grateful for his support at times when I've really needed it. He was born in Detroit the same year my parents were born in Detroit, so we have this interesting generational link too.

I don't want to think too much about the list because it's pretty intimidating. You've got a special thing going there, and I'm really looking forward to being a part of it.

Also, I have to say that these are some great, tough questions. I hope my answers do them justice. Thanks for spending the time with my work.

AK: It has been a pleasure and a privilege—as for your answers, you've done justice and then some. We're very much looking forward to your reading.

• ● •

CAROL ANN DAVIS

• ● •

Carol Ann Davis's poems have appeared in *The American Poetry Review*, *The Threepenny Review*, *Agni* and *Volt*. Her collections include *Psalm* (2007) and *Atlas Hour* (2011), which *The Los Angeles Review of Books* characterized as "unsettling, hallucinatory, ecstatic." She was awarded a fellowship in poetry from the National Endowment for the Arts, and an essay she wrote for *The Georgia Review* was named a finalist for a National Magazine Award. Davis was longtime editor of the journal *Crazyhorse*. She now edits the literary journal *Dogwood* and teaches at Fairfield University in their MFA program.

About her first collection, August Kleinzahler wrote, "There is a particular quality of quietude and stillness that suffuses these painterly poems, so involved with loss, motherhood and the shifting tonalities of light that transform the domestic and ordinary into the strange and extraordinary." About *Atlas Hour*, Sven Birkerts observed: "Carol Ann Davis works her material with a jeweler's steady hand, honoring the sensuous definition of surfaces as well as the more elusive claims of desire, sorrow and the gratitude of living. . . [In] poem after poem— there comes a catch in the breath, the sense of a rightness apprehended."

KPS READING: DECEMBER 2012

Andrew Kuhn: I understand you've recently moved up here from South Carolina. Mother Nature arranged quite a welcome. Have you and your family enjoyed the temperate Northeast so far? And did you have to leave behind *Crazyhorse*—the terrific literary magazine you ran with your husband—when you came to Fairfield University?

Carol Ann Davis: My husband and I both went to college and graduate school in the Northeast, and my husband is from Massachusetts, so we knew what we were going to be in for in terms of weather. In fact, we missed all of it all the many years we were gone, and I'm not joking when I say we feel we've come home.

Our youngest son at three years old would say, "I wish we could live where there was snow," even though he barely had any experience of snow; overhearing us over the years had affected his outlook. I would say we never lost that New England orientation. We'd drive four hours up to Asheville each fall to go apple picking and see the leaves, or drive towards rather than away from snow on the rare occasions the North Carolina mountains had it; now we go down the street for apples and see quite a leaf show from our back yard. We've already had a covering snow this fall. We love it.

We were both very sad to leave behind *Crazyhorse*, a magazine we were very involved with in many capacities for a decade, but we knew we wanted to be back in New England, and when this opportunity came up, we had to take it. *Crazyhorse* is housed at the College of Charleston and has plenty of administrative support there, so we knew we could safely depart and it would survive, which, of course, it has! We miss the magazine, but we trust we left it better for our attentions. That's really all you can hope to do.

AK: Your father was a rocket scientist. Was it fun to say that, when you were a kid, "My Daddy is a rocket scientist"? Especially right after someone said sneeringly about something, "It's not rocket science"?

CAD: Well, since I grew up proximate Kennedy Space Center, one didn't really go around bragging about one's father being a rocket scientist, since there were a fair number of other similarly situated kids around. Our rival high school was the Astronauts, a couple of towns south, where the kids of the astronauts lived who were, you can imagine, a different breed entirely from us. And my father's orientation was really that of a civil engineer. That was his training, to build roads and bridges, and then by a curious set of circumstances, he ended up being one of those guys in *Apollo 13* who was put in a room and told to square the circle (if you know the scene in the movie). I mean, literally, he was one of those guys.

My brother, who was sentient then—I was born in 1970 and missed nearly all of the good moon-mission action—told me the story of my father coming home and telling basically the same story as the one in the movie around the kitchen table. As you can imagine, it was memorable to my brother as a kid of seven or eight to have his father walk in after a sleepless night or two down at the Cape and tell him a story as amazing as that. It reminded me how consequential it all felt, those years of my family's deep involvement in the space program. Watching my father in those years definitely showed me that you could love what you do; you could serve some very ambitious purpose with the work that you chose to do, and what you do matters, all that good stuff. I have a lot of pride and affection for the happy accident of my birth into the middle of that time and into the family where I landed.

Years after my father died I was walking in Spoleto, Italy and looked down and saw a government-issue Skilcraft pen, the kind that he always wore in his pocket, the same one that thousands of U.S. civil servants of a certain era carried, black plastic with a brushed silver band. Readers who had a parent in the government will know just what I mean. It made me realize he's always with me and what a legacy being his daughter is.

But as for the "it's not rocket science" joke—not even rocket science *is* rocket science. It's amazing how practical and resourceful those guys were, how totally creative they had to be. It was a real lesson to me as a young artist: get to the moon with these materials and these limitations. Now get home. It's not that different from trying to write within limitations.

AK: Did your father's passion for rocketry and the exploration of space have anything to do with the dreamy and speculative and expansive side that comes out in your poetry?

CAD: The short answer is yes, his curiosity about the world, his desire to understand the way things work and where we are in the universe, all of that is inherited, if I have any of it in my work, and it's nice you think I might! Thank you!

He taught me celestial navigation—one of my first published poems was about that—and he always wanted NASA to go to Mars. Now that we're exploring Mars, I'm so happy; he would love it. He wanted that so badly, and to go back to the moon. So yes, I think that the idea that we are very small and our smallness is in some ways a metaphysical comfort, if that's a philosophy that undergirds the poems, it's certainly something he imparted to me. We also went on a lot of night walks at the beach (which was at the end of my street) looking up at the stars and finding the Little Dipper, the Big Dipper; all of it sort of a way of shifting and finding perspective. That informs my poetry, I think. Maybe that's the expansiveness you're talking about.

I've only just recently started to write about this time period in a conscious way, and there's a new poem in *American Poetry Review* this month of mine, about space, about that time. I think it's funny how long it takes to begin seeing your childhood inside some larger context, and mine is certainly that era. It's one of my contexts, and my father, for a lot of reasons even besides that, is a huge influence—as is natural.

Another big aspect of his life was church; I grew up Southern Baptist going to church three times a week and he was always a deacon. He was a man of science and of faith; I like that he held those two seemingly contradictory ideas in some kind of conversation, a kind of happy mystery he lived easily inside. He was tolerant of mystery—an essential aspect of poetry.

AK: Your first book of poems, *Psalm* (Tupelo Press, 2007), is a meditation on your father and his passing. Can you say a little about that collection, and what writing those poems was like for you?

CAD: Well, the collection is pretty self-explanatory: it traces a narrative arc from his death to the birth of my first child. My father died and within a year I was pregnant—in the immortal words of *Babe: Pig in the City*, the rare sequel better than the original: I was stranded. I couldn't go forward and I couldn't go back. So I wrote my way through grief, into this new experience of pregnancy.

For some weird reason, the two experiences spoke to each other. It helped me to understand both experiences to write about them. That's important, I think, to say: I write poems to better understand my life, internal and external. The poem is a by-product of trying to live mindfully. I don't know if that makes sense, but the being a good person, the living better, is the important part, and the poem is the helpmate to that.

Writing these poems basically got me through that time. Looking back at those poems I can see some of what I was going through; at the time I didn't know and couldn't have told you. I can make sense of the poems in retrospect but at the time I felt I was wrestling with unknowns.

AK: Your most recent collection is called *Atlas Hour* (Tupelo Press, 2011). The poem by that title starts by intimating a kind of post-disaster landscape (beginning as it does "the flood that passed"). There's a suggestion that a further and more final apocalypse may be imminent ("*the zero hour   is upon us*") and that the thing to do in response is to "*submit*" (emphases in original).

All this in the first five lines! But then things take a turn for the more domestic and seemingly benign. The children, though bitten, (apparently only by some kind of bug), are asleep, and the "*finally*" suggests that the poet, who is also a parent, is preoccupied with the ordinary hassles associated with that role, rather than with the end of the world as she knows it. Can you talk a little about what this poem means to you, where its title comes from, and why you made it your title poem?

CAD: I just came up with the title. I liked the way the words sounded together, atlas and hour, and later it seemed to be a fitting title for the whole collection. The idea of an atlas, a book of the world, combined with the hour in which it is read, the hour you spend with it, a kind of pure attention. In a way, it's a more fitting title for the collection than for the poem.

The poem itself is a little bit strange, and I've never really thought of this poem as having a "post-disaster landscape," but that's one of the great gifts of sending your poems out into the world. The echo that comes back (the feedback, as the sound an amp gives to a guitar) is wildly interesting. I love hearing your description of the poem—I almost feel it needs no answer because the question you're asking has its own sense, the sense of the reader who must read the poem alone, without the poet for notes and annotations.

There's something pure in that exchange that the poet sullies by commenting. Inside that moment, for the reader (who, as I've said in the previous answer, isn't a concern for me as I write the poem because I am concerned only with what I can learn from the poem) the poem is best if it is both clear and open. Clear as in followable, not needlessly opaque, and open as in open to the reader's interacting with it, as you have here.

So in a way I don't know what I can say about the poem besides that I like how you read it and it adds some dimension to it to hear you think about it.

When I wrote the poem it was a poem concerned with the wilderness of parenthood, and it's addressing my husband about this joint venture of the children in a sort of intimate shorthand of a type I was very keen on in exploring the book. Specifically to address this poem, though, so much is at stake in the day to day of parenthood, but half the time you are just preoccupied with things like bug bites. And you're never sure when the children were bitten or by what, or when they'll fall asleep. The proof of your existence is simply their existence; it's terrifying and miraculous.

In a lot of ways—practical and spiritual—you're hostage to the ups and downs of it, or it feels that way, especially in the early years. This poem interacts with that feeling. I think it takes place on the porch of our old apartment after a storm; it was a great wide porch, and

Charleston had some great storms. That's the post-disaster part, which is just the calm after a thunderstorm of the sort that happen there. Of course it's easy to be sentimental about such storms once you're out of them, as I am now; the poem is closer to that time than I am now and so it bathes me in that for the time I read it.

AK: The poems in *Atlas Hour* have a tranquil presentation, maybe because of the spacing on the page of multiple short phrases, which seem to balance each other, or to move serenely along like leaves in a current, or like thoughts during meditation—they are there, the reader notices them for a moment, then has to let them go. A flood and a child's watercolor are stressed about the same. But there's a lot of dark material, even in the ekphrastic pieces, the poems that take their inspiration from and comment upon works of art.

CAD: First I must say you're generous to use words like "tranquil" and "serene" to describe the form; I think many readers find the spacing anything but! Still, as I said before, I was writing to discover something, and the form just helped me with that, which is why I used it.

This is by way of explanation, which I realize you haven't asked for, but many have felt the form was hard to enter, and so I just want to say that I entered the form because it welcomed me—and I hope it welcomes the reader, although the reader has to sort of leave some expectations about clarity, I suppose, or regular narrative pacing, at the door of the poem. The reader has to, as it were, take off his or her shoes to enter, or as Wittgenstein says—I'm paraphrasing—one must climb the ladder and then throw it away. If the form requires some sort of supplication from the reader, I hope he or she is reassured that it first required the same thing of me!

I realized after I worked with the form for a while that it was increasing the intimacy level in the poem. As I said about "Atlas Hour," I was able to talk in a sort of shorthand to my husband; likewise to my children, and eventually, to artists, and even to events, such as suicides and genocides. The dark material came in—I don't know how else to say it—quite naturally once the form was doing its work on me. It's as if the form itself, its engagement with language, its weird clarity, asked more of me as a human being.

And so as a human being some of these larger issues (the nature of violence, how suffering happens, what it means to bear witness, etc.) became accessible to me through my experimentation with language and form. It seems, I think, like a wild leap to go from parenthood to genocide, but if you think about it, it's not. Plenty of parents have found themselves in such situations; it's just an accident of my circumstance that I haven't. And that others have, has something to do with me. I don't know if that makes much good sense, but it's all I can do to explain it.

AK: Sometimes the contrast between what you're writing about and the way you're writing about it is startling, almost eerie. "Upon Seeing the Terezin Children's Drawings, Two Parts" references a collection of drawings done by children in a transfer camp outside Prague during the Holocaust. The approach in the poem to this situation and material is oblique, and the references to the central situation and the people seemingly muted. Can you say a little bit about how this poem came to be, and how you would want us to engage and understand it?

CAD: My first engagement is with tone, with the tone of the language that is coming to me, and then within that I will engage—obliquely or directly as the tone requires—with the body of knowledge, with the subject, as it were, of the poem. But it's sort of secondary to the tonal color, and that poem in particular runs almost entirely on tone.

I had been to Prague with my husband many years earlier and then we visited again when our children were very small. On both occasions we visited the children's drawings described in the poem that are housed at The Jewish Museum in Prague. The second time I saw them my second son was four months old and strapped to my body as I walked through, which I remember feeling was deeply ironic, the weight of him, his nearness, surrounded by the art of these exterminated children.

I can't in all honesty say I ever thought I would write about it—at the time I'm certain I felt I would not ever have "a right" to do so—it was just an experience that stayed with me. Then, a year or two later after this form had progressed a bit for me I found myself writing about that experience, and I just let the poem do its work on me. I took details from that time—such as an altarpiece called *Christ in Limbo* we had seen shortly before—and I sort of let the thing knit together.

Then, as I often do, I flipped the poem to see what would happen to the sequence of ideas. And something very strange happened: a really emphatic energy unleashed in the second half. I could see it was compelling and I just left it as it fell. Usually when I flip a poem I keep only the second half, but here it felt right to make it a mirror poem, to revisit everything once the world was turned upside down, as it had been for the children.

But the engine under the poem is the parents, these parents who had art classes for their children in a camp. These parents decided to have their children continue to process their worlds through artistic expression; I find it deeply moving and heroic that they did this. I can't think of anything more difficult or beautiful than what they gave their children by collectively teaching those classes in that setting. What must that have been like?

AK: Your first collection was called *Psalm* and some of your work in *Atlas Hour* is overtly prayerful. Even the Terezin poem references "the story of the annunciation" and *Christ in Limbo*. Do you consider yourself a spiritual poet, and is yours a specifically Christian spirituality?

CAD: This has come up a bit, especially in the reviews of *Atlas Hour*. *Psalm*, dedicated to my father, was a direct homage to my upbringing in the Baptist Church, of which I've not been a member my entire adult life. As an adult I am deeply agnostic, though I don't like the word spiritual very much, since I like the ritual of religion.

Well, this is getting a little muddy. Perhaps biography can help: I grew up reading the Bible, and I had an influential preacher with whom my family was very close—he was also the chaplain for the Daytona

International Speedway and a visual artist and musician as well, a very interesting presence in my life. From an early age artistic practice and religion have been joined, just as science is not so separated from religion in my father's thinking. I don't remember a lot of big lines being drawn between these aspects of my life, and all of them feel like formative experiences to me.

So yes, it's a short walk from that upbringing to an interest in devotional art, which is where things like the Annunciation come into the poems. My interest in visual art reaches its apotheosis in someone like Fra Angelico, who is bringing a bunch of areas of inquiry together for me in his art. Whenever the Annunciation is mentioned, his frescoes aren't far behind in my thinking.

But also, as I said, in the "Terezin" poem I just grabbed around for the details of that day, the things we had seen around the same time (such as the "courtyard full of bees" outside our apartment), and we had just gone to a medieval art museum and seen these amazing altar pieces, not just *Christ in Limbo* but *Our Lady of Sorrows* and several others. I love every bit of it—the wood of the altarpiece, the paint, the language—it's a joining of all my essential interests.

So in terms of language and form I'm mixing some of this together, all of these felt experiences, that are real but not necessarily sequential or related, and I'm seeing how the tone of one thing runs up against another; then I'm also, as you said earlier, "leveling" the importance of each of them. In the moment of experiencing them, they're all important, all equal.

I think I do that because as we perceive the world we don't know, immediately, what is more important than something else. Importance is assigned in retrospect, and I'm not interested in making explicit meanings exactly. I'm much more interested in feeling it than knowing it.

So when I'm writing, I don't add value and importance as a habit. A true exploration depends, I guess, on not judging what you're seeing as important or unimportant. I try to keep an open mind, and I hope that means I get to see a little bit more of the visual field, a little bit more of the periphery.

AK: How has your experience of being a parent changed you as a poet?

CAD: It's almost ridiculous to answer. It has totally changed me. When my oldest was born, my sister said something to me like, "Here he is. The one who changes everything." And she was absolutely right. I'm so lucky they're here.

AK: Looking at the list of writers who have read for our series, do you see any names of poets who have influenced your own development?

CAD: Well, it's such an incredibly esteemed series, I kind of can't believe I'm a part of it. So it's humbling to imagine my name will join that list in a few short weeks, and it would take me years to explain how so many of the poets on the list have influenced me or helped my thinking about poems.

But I'd be remiss not to mention that the person who has most influenced me—among an embarrassment of riches on your list—is my own teacher, James Tate. It's no understatement to say that he gave my poetry life to me. I will live all my days inside the bright light of that great debt.

• ● •

MICHAEL DICKMAN

• • •

Michael Dickman grew up near Portland, Oregon with his mother and twin brother, Matthew, also a poet. His collection *Flies* (2011) won the James Laughlin Award from the Academy of American Poets. Subsequent to reading for the Series, Michael and his brother Matthew released a book of poems, *Brother*, about the suicide of their half-brother.

In his young career, Dickman has garnered much interest and praise. Of his first collection, *The End of the West* (2009), Dominic Luxford noted, "Elizabeth Bishop said that the three qualities she admired most in poetry were accuracy, spontaneity, and mystery. Michael Dickman's first full-length collection of poems demonstrates each brilliantly." In *The New Yorker*, Rebecca Mead characterized his poems as "interior, fragmentary, and austere, often stripped down to single-word lines; they seethe with incipient violence." A reviewer in *Rattle* noted "*Flies* is one of the rare books of poetry I couldn't put down until I finished it. The book is surreal, engaging, and strikes a consistent tone . . . a book worth reading, contemplating, arguing, and agreeing with."

KPS READING: MARCH 2013

Andrew Kuhn: I promise that the first question I ask about you will not also be about your twin brother Matthew the poet.

Your first collection is named *Flies* (Copper Canyon Press), your second is *The End of the West* (Copper Canyon). Various kinds of mortality have been much on your mind, it seems. Can you say a little about that?

Michael Dickman: I should say that I'd be happy to talk about the poet Matthew Dickman. Though, as a twin, I bow to your attempt to address me as an individual. Our whole lives Matthew and I received, for example, the same birthday cards, so neither one would be jealous. So thank you, from the start, for not seeing double.

Now might be a good time to point out that *Flies* is my second book, from 2011. *The End of the West* is my first book, from 2009. I do think this matters, perhaps in very small ways or details, or perhaps just to me, in that I feel like *Flies* stretches out lyrically from *TEOTW*. In some ways *Flies* is also less concerned with a strong forward narrative. I hope the poems in *Flies* move more in increments, little by little, image by image.

I wonder if this business with mortality that you see has to do with my being brought up in Catholic school? Could be. Most likely, though, it's not for me to say.

AK: Sorry for that boneheaded error! Usually I know that 2009 comes *before* 2011.

I understand that you're a new papa—for which, congratulations. Besides depriving you of sleep, has this event had any immediate effect on your writing? Or on your take on mortality and ways to subvert it?

MD: Thanks for the kind word about the Little One. It's true; I am now someone's dad. I didn't grow up with a dad, so it is a wild and amazing thing to be one. The immediate effect on my writing is that I'm not writing anything. But soon, soon. I can feel it. As for subverting mortality, I was taught that we couldn't. I like that about mortality: it's here to stay, even if we're not.

AK: In *Flies* you sell the reader surrealist premises with very matter-of-fact language and images that for the most part scan with great visual precision. Were you ever a fan of magical realism? Are you self-consciously or intentionally surrealist—do you have surrealist heroes—or is that just the way your mind tends to move?

MD: Well, damn, I'm going to have to take what my grandmother calls umbrage with your use of the word "sell." I don't think any poet is trying to SELL anyone anything. I'm certainly not. At least I don't think I am. We are sold things by advertisers, small interest groups, and politicians of every stripe. But poets? Which ones?

Now this will sound like I'm being coy, or just dim, but I don't think of the poems in *Flies* as being surreal. I understand that things happen in the poems that don't seem to happen in the actual world. Though, for me, it all was true. My older brother died. I was visited by flies. Emotionally and spiritually and physically, all those poems happened just as they are. And so I guess it's just the way my mind moves, like you say, and it moves that way because it's how I experience the world.

AK: The Portland, Oregon that figures in your poems is not the gateway-to-fabulous-outdoor-recreation or hilariously politically "Portlandia" kind of place the casual outsider might picture. [*NB: "Portlandia" is a satirical cable TV series.*] It sounds pretty brutal, and it becomes clear in your poetry that a good number of the people you grew up with didn't make it. Can you talk a little bit about the Portland you knew? What were some things that made it possible for you not only to survive, but to thrive?

MD: Portland as a gateway to truly awesome and beautiful natural places was always a reality, and we did make it to the Oregon coast every summer for a couple weeks. The mountains and the forests were more of a mystery to me. I grew up in a working class neighborhood that I loved. I didn't experience it as brutal. But it was a hard place at times. That said, it was also a tight community. We all knew our neighbors. The Portland I knew growing up was more Gus Van Sant than "Portlandia." And I wouldn't change a thing. I was able to thrive because of my family, and a small handful of friends, and a couple very important mentors. A lucky childhood.

AK: "From the Lives of My Friends" is a very spare, three-part collective elegy that includes some strange lines:

> My friends and I climbed up the telephone poles to sit on the
> powerlines dressed like crows

> Their voices sounded like lemons

I won't ask what a lemon sounds like to you. That last line makes me wonder if you ever went through a *Mad Libs* period. Do you approach writing poetry, at least in part, in the spirit of pure play?

MD: I remember *Mad Libs*, though I don't think I could make a poem that way. And I do think that a lot of poetry is play. Serious play. High stakes play. But sure, play all the same.

But I wonder what the opposite of a strange line is for you? There can be, I hope, a kind of sense in a poem that is strictly musical, or tonal, or that stays partially hidden and I think that's all right. Has to be. There is a lot out there that I think is strange, but I like those things. A star-nosed mole is pretty strange. A platypus is strange. Photosynthesis. A little strange. Okay, now I'm coming out for the strange things of the world to unite and take over. Let your freak flag fly!

AK: Your poetry has a considerable amount of Christian imagery and references, much of it set in an unorthodox context, with even less orthodox or even frankly profane content. You mentioned being brought up in a Catholic school. I guess organized religion played a major role in your upbringing?

MD: The Episcopal and Catholic churches played a big role in my upbringing as my mother kept us in Catholic school from first grade through high school. We attended Mass on the weekends and went to Sunday school. I was an altar-boy. And so those stories and images made their way under my skin. Deeply, deeply. Somewhere the great poet Charles Wright says something about the images we grow up with being the images we are stuck with. I think that's right.

AK: "Stations," for example, has prominent echoes of the Stations of the Cross. There are fourteen parts to the poem, instead of the conventional twelve, but in broad outline the poem tracks with what you would find depicted in stained glass in a church.

At the fourth station, Jesus encounters his mother. Your fourth stanza begins,

> You will meet once again in perfection your mother on the street
>   but you will not recognize her

Two lines later, though, sexual partners are talking dirty with each other. One of them has to remind himself,

> Thank god you're not my mother

> You're not my mother

as if he weren't altogether sure. Besides giving aid and comfort to the beaten-up Freudians amongst us, who can use it, these juxtapositions are funny and tender and moving. And the movement from the sacred to the profane is not one-way; immediately after the lines quoted above comes this startling affirmation:

> From moment to moment God is the one pressing us against the
>   glorious metal shining everywhere in the universe

> Except when from moment to moment we are

Do you think of yourself as a religious person, or as a religious poet?

MD: First off I need to point out that there are *fourteen* Stations and not, as you say, twelve. I hope you won't mind the corrective, but if I let it go I'm afraid the sisters from Our Lady of Sorrows would fly out to New Jersey to rap me on the knuckles. Besides if you leave out the last two stations some would accuse you of leaving out the most important and redemptive part for our life on earth.

AK: Bonehead error number two! One more and I'm out.

MD: Not at all. Perhaps we'd be better off with fewer of them. I'll also point out that this poem is a response, though a secret one, to a series of paintings by Barnett Newman. Do you know them?

AK: Not before reading *Flies*. The poem placed just before "Stations" in your book is "Barnett Newman: Black Fire I." But I didn't pick up that "Stations" also referred to his work.

MD: He made them first and then titled them afterwards, which seems like a great description of religious experience to me.

I am not a religious person except in the sense that I stand in awe of the natural world and in awe and anger and wonder at our relationship to it and to each other. I don't pray. I don't go to church. And I don't think of my poems as being religious or myself as a religious poet. It's too hard to just get a couple lines down. I don't think I could do it if I thought I had a spiritual or cultural mandate or call as well.

AK: You bang up against the problem of evil very hard in "Late Meditation."

> Yesterday we put all our kids in the car, doused it with gasoline,
> and lit it on fire

In the poem this horror seems to come out of nowhere, a narrative punch in the face. It's such a shocking incident that it sounds like something specific that actually happened. Is it, or is it a kind of model of the awfulness the species is capable of?

MD: We can safely say that that moment is an example of the horror we are capable of.

AK: The "we" in this poem seems to implicate the reader. The speaker seems to be trying to quiet his mind, ultimately unsuccessfully. By the end, the whole enterprise of meditation is made to look paltry at best in the face of atrocity. There seems to be a movement in both collections from qualified hope and affirmation to moments of despair, and then back again. Is this a way that you experience life and the world as you walk around, or is it an intensification that comes particularly when you're writing?

MD: I really like your word intensification. I think it's true that sitting down to write a poem brings with it, for me at least (and I know I'm not alone!), a kind of intensity, a feeling of being tuned up, a slight sense of weight. Though I hope the poems aren't HEAVY. Or at least not unrelentingly so. I think there are little moments of release in the poems, if just in the white space around the strophes.

AK: You use quite a few four-letter words in your poems—maybe not more, on a statistical basis, than a lot of people use in conversation, but more than one usually finds in a volume of poems. Do four-letter words provide a certain kind of charge that's not available otherwise? Or are they so ubiquitous now that keeping them out of a poem would just seem silly?

MD: I think they are ubiquitous. And they are Language, and Individual, and so do things other language doesn't. It makes it hard for my 98-year-old Grandma to read, but frankly her ears aren't really burning...though she may pretend they are.

AK: The cover of *The End of the West* is a ghostly photo by Ralph Eugene Meatyard of a blurred figure in white jumping up or down before an empty, darkened window frame of an old brick building. In

HOW A POEM CAN HAPPEN

Flies, you have an ekphrastic poem—"Ralph Eugene Meatyard: Untitled"—that takes off from an actual or imagined photograph. Can you say a little about how this photographer's work speaks to you?

MD: Ralph Eugene Meatyard. Was there a better American photographer of the strangeness of childhood? Maybe, but I don't know who it is. His photographs have been a meditation and lightning rod for me. His photos of trees seemed more like trees to me than Ansel Adams's work, and his use of masks feel like live theater. He was also a great friend to many poets, including Wendell Berry and Denise Levertov, for example. And Guy Davenport and Jonathan Williams, for another. And I like that. I wish someone like Meatyard would come spend time at my house. Have a few drinks. Listen to some music.

AK: Your twin brother Matthew also writes excellent poetry, but astonishingly, it is not identical to your own poetry! How do you account for this?

MD: I bow to your curiosity and wonder with this question. But frankly I don't find it astonishing. Why would you expect identical twins to do identical work and not, say, siblings with a couple years between them? Though we look alike we have managed to find our own ways in the world, though we are entwined at our roots. It must have happened in utero! And perhaps our very different poetry is a subconscious self-defense against disappearing in the shadow of the other brother? I account for it in the same way any family members who find themselves in the same business would.

AK: You vary your line lengths quite a bit, and your poems are spare on the page, with a lot of space. Your brother favors long lines and dense blocks of text, and a more consistently ecstatic or at least celebratory tone that for me, at least, evokes Whitman and Ginsberg. Do the differences in your poetry reflect differences in temperament that were present even before you started writing poetry?

MD: Not that I can see. You know, it's not as if Matthew is gregarious and socially outgoing and I am quiet and spare in my friendships. I think as different artists we were pulled to different things, styles, obsessions, different ways of seeing and singing what I hope are our particular songs. I don't think temperament has much to do with what an artist makes.

Of course it can—Pollock dripping his ecstatic life away and Newman in a bowtie making zips, for example. Still, Samuel Beckett was a funny and outgoing correspondent who kept hundreds of vibrant friendships, which may not be reflected in the plays or fiction. I mean, *Nohow On* does not come out very far to shake our hand, though the author would have.

AK: Looking at the list of our readers over the past four-plus decades, are there any who stand out as particular influences of yours?

MD: Thanks for taking the time to ask these questions. If any of my answers sound too brief or foggy we should chalk it up to new parenthood.

I want to say it's a lucky thing to be asked to read in public. And a series like this makes it very exciting. You know, every third poet who's read for this series has been an influence on me in one way or another. So I'll just say that my most recent influence is John Clare. A mud-man punk rocker from the 1800s. All I want to do these days is write a poem about a bird's nest, all because of him.

• ● •

JESSICA GREENBAUM

• ● •

Jessica Greenbaum's *The Two Yvonnes* (2012) was chosen by Paul Muldoon for Princeton's Series of Contemporary Poets. She lives in Brooklyn, where some of her poems are set; others hail from the Bronx, Long Island, Houston and stranger, less readily identifiable locales. Ms. Greenbaum is the poetry editor of *upstreet*. Her poetry has appeared in *The New Yorker* and *Poetry* and over fifty other venues. In 2015 she received a National Endowment for the Arts Literary Award, and in 2016 the Poetry Society of America's Agnes Fay di Castagnola Award. She has taught at Manhattanville College, Pratt, and her alma mater, Barnard. A trained social worker, Greenbaum has also led workshops for The World Trade Center Health Program for First Responders.

Of her first collection, *Inventing Difficulty* (2000), which won the Gerald Cable award for a first book of poetry, George Steiner wrote, "A sinewy, vividly intelligent humanity gives to this collection its memorable voice. In one sense, Jessica Greenbaum's poems are incisively local, that Brooklyn landscape out of Whitman and Hart Crane. In another sense, however, they tell of the larger sadness and recognitions of our century. . . . A first book by a poet very much to be listened to."

KPS READING: SEPTEMBER 2015

Andrew Kuhn: You grew up on Long Island and sojourned in Houston for seven years as a reporter. How did your time as a journalist down south affect your development as a person and a poet? Anything about telling a story swiftly, economically, pared to the essentials?

Jessica Greenbaum: Andy, thanks for this question, because my apprenticeship in journalism came at the right time for me, and I have often wondered about the dialectic between these practices. I had the misfortune of feeling limited by the job board at the University of Houston where, in 1979, I was in the very first class of their creative writing program. So I snuck into Rice University's job center and applied to be a researcher/reporter for the *Forbes* Houston bureau.

Then I had the good fortune of being hired based on the fact that I had snuck in somewhere—as all reporters should be able to do! And further, to be mentored by one of the great journalists I have known—William Baldwin, who went on to become the executive editor of the whole magazine for decades to come.

I once told him I was flummoxed because a line of mine had been filched from a poem of mine and appeared in *The Nation*. He asked me how much they paid, took out his calculator, hit a few buttons, pulled up the tape and said, "The guy owes you a quarter."

Yes, I learned about economy (both kinds), details, story progression, and a good bit about business (although I never really grokked it enough—I once tipped my hand and asked a CEO what amortization really means). Overall, I felt I was learning how the dots were connected in the world—and behind the world's facade. The Houston writing program at the time was an emotional desert for me—I got about zero encouragement. So as my peers were all being published and being selected to attend AWP, in between poems I was journeying to Jackson, Mississippi to write catfish stories, filing Standard & Poor's reports, and happily depositing a paycheck. And we never do know when we are going to have *those* on a steady basis. I became permanently admiring of the profession and very little is as moving to me as the work of those journalists who change the world through investigative reporting. And, at this point, often risk their lives . . .

AK: Since coming back north, you've made the city, specifically Brooklyn, your home for thirty years or so. Your work evokes the city with great sharpness and affection, even in its grittier, disorienting guises, as in "We Want the Hurricane."

> . . . . We want the hurricane
> Because it had been a summer of car trouble, plumbers
> And broken typewriters (once three to a room!),
> Of the toothy keys which just make worse our own
> Inability to say goodbye. This summer we are at the mercy
> Of machines, praying for the air conditioning and more
> Prey to all the harshness of the town which rises
> Then bears down, sun without a parasol,
> Like the world was wool and you had to wear beneath it,
> . . . . we want
> The hurricane to shut this city down.

[From *Inventing Difficulty*, 2000]

Despite its hassles and harshness, what about the city drew you back, as an adult, to stay? What makes it a particularly compelling setting and subject for your poetry?

JG: Andy, that poem is about Houston . . . but how could you know that?

I was born in Brooklyn, and because I returned to Manhattan (where I had gone to college) for a research job for the civil rights division of the Anti-Defamation League, I happened to be able to move into my grandmother's apartment in the Hasidic part of Williamsburg when she moved out. Especially after the general disenfranchisement of my Texas years, moving into that native, well-loved home definitely clinched the deal.

There was the miniature wooden piano that held a spool inside, her chair next to the phone table, a drawer with packs of Beemans gum! But I like your word "compelled," because that does say it—I am drawn to the mix of streets and culture, of botanic gardens and general mayhem. And I have the good fortune of being able to get OUT every now and again . . . which, let's face it, is nearly a prerequisite luxury in order to love the place. Then the skyline comes into view upon a return and everything feels A-okay.

AK: You studied with Kenneth Koch in your early days; he also wrote vividly of the city, and was associated with the poets loosely described as "the New York School.". . . Like you, too, he taught poetry in innovative ways and in places it's not typically found. Was he a lasting influence, or were those affinities and paths you would have come to on your own?

JG: Koch—along with Marilyn Hacker, and Bill Zavatsky, with whom I also studied as an undergraduate—remains a treasured coach in the mental dugout. Thank goodness I was in the foamy wake of the New York School with all its candor, humor, irreverence, narrative and humanism. I am still friends with poets from that year-long class— Stephen Ackerman, Daniel Meltz, Jeffrey Harrison—and Koch's penultimate book, *New Addresses*, continues to present itself to me as the book I wish I had written or could write, might perhaps approach kind-of-like almost writing . . .

AK: I understand you recently got your master's degree in social work, establishing forever your credentials as "a lifelong learner," as if being a poet weren't enough in that regard. Can you say a little about that experience, why you did it, and how it relates if at all to your practice and teaching of poetry?

JG: Nice to talk about social work. First, I guess: art just can't do everything. I want to be able to throw my puny weight against the massive wall of various difficulties . . . for what it's worth. I have an interest in the field called Narrative Medicine and I was invited to teach a workshop for 9/11 first responders through the World Trade Center's 9/11 Health Program, which was kind of dream come true as I have always wanted to work with the police and firefighters.

We had a great time, and part of what's satisfying is how the discipline of writing poems—observation of outer and inner worlds—can be meaningful to people suffering from PTSD. If you can be here now, you can move back a bit from the movie of trauma that interferes with a full life. That's a shorthand, but I hope it answers a bit. I am immersing myself in a study about trauma with the head of that program and hoping to apply for funds so that we can continue. I'm also collaborating with a more senior social worker on starting a group for parents of adult children with chronic mental health issues, and our group will also include a writing component. Like the 9/11 workshop, the writing won't focus on the issue—it will focus on the imagination.

AK: You've published two collections of poetry, *Inventing Difficulty* (Silverfish Review Press, 1998) and *The Two Yvonnes* (Princeton University Press, 2012). In many of your poems, there is an intimacy of address that is disarming. Still, I was startled, looking at the notes at the end of each one, by how many of them carry dedications to specific people. Is that often how a poem starts for you, as a continuation or an intensification of a conversation with someone in particular?

JG: Life is with people, as a famous book about *shtetl* life says. Some of those poems are direct addresses to the dedicatees . . . and, as you so respectfully put it, part of an ongoing conversation. But others are just offerings . . . because I am so often comforted by the empathy and accompaniment of my friends in this loony human condition thing.

AK: Are there people in your life who have expressed that they're a little put out that they haven't yet rated a dedicated poem?

JG: Ha ha! I do worry that the list looks egregious . . . oh well!

AK: As vividly as your "Hurricane" poem, from the first collection, evokes a city's "climate / of persistent agitation," your later work has more often found its way to a grateful, celebratory note, which some-

times and seemingly quite self-consciously adopts some of the language
and the attitudes of prayer. Not that the path to such affirmations is
presented as an easy one, in fact anything but. In "Beauty's Rearrange-
ments" the narrator is in the existential deep-end from the very first
stanza, but is rescued by the city, this time in an unexpected guise.

> I had been thinking about everything being
> relative, especially our considerations
> of joy and grief,
>
> which led me to thinking about the universe,
> and not finding any other planet like ours
> within light-years
>
> and other units of distance— which themselves
> have no beginning but tend toward
> bunches of billions—
>
> my mind picked up on where it had left off fraying.
> Thankfully my god of reconciliation
> (New York City)
>
> collects string, sometimes tying it together. . . .

From the abstract, anxious ruminations of the first stanza, in which
the expanding universe seems to be flying apart inside the narrator, her
interaction with her daughter in a most marvelous yarn shop brings
her back down to earth, with a seemingly miraculous transformation
of one strong feeling into its opposite.

> And, here, I racked
>
> my brain for up and down, where might the universe
> hold us in regard, because sometimes
> our joyous combinations
>
> turn renegade, like the runaway Pleiades, or our
> idyllic summers play in other hemispheres
> as grievously cold,

but when the yarn was handed over still charged
with transformation and no strand was
left to fall alone

I saw my eight-year-old delighted by the task
of beauty's rearrangements, and let my
sorrows spin to gold.

[From *The Two Yvonnes: Poems*, 2012]

So . . . what's my question? Besides "How do you do that?"—meaning, for example, just how do you stitch the cosmic to the quotidian so seamlessly, a question to which no one could reasonably expect an answer—what do you think accounts for the increased ability and/or willingness of your narrator—you?—to achieve a more or less hard-won stance of hopefulness? Anything to do with the experience of being a parent?

JG: I'm not trying to flatter you but you flatter *me*—these are the most generous questions ever. I think my particular filters for experience include both poems and personal essays . . . and having been taught to essay out—to wander—-by the teachings and writings of Phillip Lopate, I tend to want to try to see how this whole show coheres. Melville writes that the inner construction of the whaleboat resembles the skeleton of the whale itself, and that notion—and the three thousand others like it in *Moby Dick*—really do speak a language in which I am having a conversation with life.

AK: Elsewhere you've cited D. Nurkse as one of your two favorite Brooklyn poets (the other being Walt Whitman), so I know that you're both familiar with and fond of at least one of our recent readers. Looking at the list of poets who have read for the Katonah Poetry Series, do you see any others who have been influential on your development?

JG: Oh my gosh, I just looked at this list. Well, every fourth poet. But because it's a fun party game, I'll just mention some of the women whose voices I especially hear in my head: Bass, Hadas, Muske-Dukes, Olds, Ponsot, Rukeyser. But just looking at this list reveals such treasures! For each of those poets I wanted to mention specific poems, and then the same for thirty others. Thank you for such a collection of favorites. It's a reminder of what we have.

• ● •

MATTHEA HARVEY

•●•

Matthea Harvey is either seriously playful or playfully serious, but however you slice it her sense of humor is wicked, as might be guessed from the titles of some of her collections: *Pity the Bathtub Its Forced Embrace of the Human Form* (2000), *Sad Little Breathing Machine* (2004), and *If the Tabloids Are True What Are You?* (2014). She experiments with erasure and collaboration with visual artists—see *Of Lamb* (2011)—and writes poems for adults about mermaids and talking animals in a book that includes photos of sculpture (*If the Tabloids*). Music, too, is woven into her work, as are fables, the history of technology, oblique takes on how our society processes terror, and startling episodes of gruesome whimsy. Harvey has also published two illustrated children's books: *The Little General and the Giant Snowflake* and *Cecil the Pet Glacier*.

A recipient of the Kingsley Tufts Poetry Award and contributing editor to *jubilat* and *BOMB*, she has taught at Sarah Lawrence, the Pratt Institute, and the Iowa Writer's Workshop. Of her collection *Modern Life* (2007), reviewer David Orr writes, "Harvey's poetry becomes a glass through which we can perceive, darkly, an even greater darkness."

KPS READING: NOVEMBER 2011

Andrew Kuhn: Your poetry is such an unusual and delightful combination of airy and dense, fantastical and down-to-earth. You present surreal situations matter-of-factly, with great specificity and assurance. The choices do not feel arbitrary, but seem to have the logic of a dream— not as a dream is told, but as it's dreamed. How do you do that?

Matthea Harvey: Well, sometimes the poems are inspired by dream, but probably only 1 in 20. Generally, I start with one idea, say, "What would a museum of the middle look like and why might it exist?" and then the details invent themselves from there. They are imagined worlds, but I think of them as fully real and hopefully that comes through in the writing.

AK: If you don't mind, I'm going to refer to specific previously published poems of yours that you have generously made available online. The poem "Setting the Table" is a kind of bent how-to, which in a very authoritative voice describes some strange procedures—it reads a little like Martha Stewart on mushrooms. Do you ever laugh out loud when you're writing?

MH: Not usually—I've blushed and I've cried, but I did laugh out loud at the idea of Martha Stewart on mushrooms! Funnily enough, I have *Martha Stewart's Encyclopedia of Crafts* on my desk, which has some great sections: "How to Punch Fabric Flowers" sounds like the beginning of a poem and there's even a "Glitter Glossary!" I have yet to do any of these projects, but I like to think one day I might.

I did laugh recently when I was writing a new mermaid poem on the train to D.C. ("The Objectified Mermaid") and I had her say that the photographer was treating her like a "spork." That was my first foray into hybrid tools, and I was kind of delighted by it. I need to seek out some others . . . the fabulous "knoon" or knife-spoon.

AK: In many of your poems, in a short space you create alternate realities that are compelling and in some cases quite disturbing. The poem "Implications for Modern Life" is almost enough to make one consider becoming a vegetarian. It's not even so much the images, which I found every bit as creepy as anything in Buñuel, but the aura of bad conscience pervading the whole piece. Is that an effect you were going for at the outset, or did it just emerge from the material?

MH: That poem was inspired by a particularly disturbing dream and as I was writing it, the sense of responsibility for creating this imagery started to come into the poem. That surprised me. In a way, though, I'm surprised that hadn't come into my poems earlier, since I do invent these creatures and people and put them in pretty dreadful situations. I didn't want to inhabit that landscape of platelets and ham—why should a reader?

AK: There's so much that's playful yet quite mordant in your work—it's right there in the titles of two of your collections, *Pity the Bathtub Its Forced Embrace of the Human Form* (Alice James Books, 2002), and *Sad Little Breathing Machine* (Graywolf Press, 2004). You mess around shamelessly with words—you were the first to put "rapture" and "rupture" in adjoining lines, I believe—but there's a certain austerity of attitude even in your jokes, it seems. "We practice drawing cubes—/ That's the house squared away." Some of your poems read a little like Lewis Carroll or Ogden Nash by way of Poe. Have you ever had a weakness for any of those writers?

MH: Absolutely. I love Ogden Nash, Lewis Carroll, and Edward Gorey (I just read a collection of his letters to Peter Neumeyer—oh to have received those decorated envelopes . . .). Poe less so. The wordplay in Nash's poems is so delicious—this is one of my favorites:

The Shrimp

A shrimp who sought his lady shrimp
Could catch no glimpse
Not even a glimp.
At times, translucence
Is rather a nuisance.

I haven't, however, written any poetry for children. My two children's books (*The Little General and the Giant Snowflake* and the forthcoming *Cecil, the Pet Glacier*) are both in prose. My poems are playful, but usually underneath the play is something quite dark or sad—a shark, or a razor blade. I'm not sure why I'm more optimistic in my prose, but so far that has been the case.

AK: Sentimentality is almost a third rail in poetry nowadays, and you seem to touch on the topic in a delightfully oblique way in "The Gem is on Page Sixty-Four." You write, "Sentimental outbreaks were not uncommon & there were crews / Trained in containment but they could never predict the next / One." This in a kind of dystopia where it seems we're meant to identify with the rebels and not the containment crews.

But you could be called pretty rigorously unsentimental yourself. In "The Crowd Cheered as Gloom Galloped Away," you take the most flagrantly sentimental artifacts—pretty, miniature ponies—pair them with psycho-pharmaceutical packaging, and subject them to terrible abuse, even unto being devoured by rats. (This poem should carry a warning label, *Do Not Read to Eight-Year-Old Girls*). Even more subversively, in "Ideas Go Only So Far" you flout the sentimental conventions of motherhood by inventing a baby that's machine-washable, although as it turns out, not indefinitely. Have you no heart? Or do you mistrust your readers' hearts, in their gooier manifestations?

MH: No one's asked me that before! I do have a heart, it's just small, black and made out of velvet.

In the first poem you mention, I'm definitely on the side of the sentimentalists, but I'm not a Hallmark aficionado. I don't think about whether my readers are sentimental or not—probably like me, there are things that reduce them to a puddle of goo and things that leave them cold. I'm very sentimental about animals—I can't bear to see them die (so, sadly, I couldn't watch the amazing series "Planet Earth"—too much weeping when the polar bear begins to starve), so writing the poem about the tiny ponies was hard.

I felt bad about killing the baby, too—I particularly liked her incarnation as a "peacefully blinking footstool"— that would be a useful and soothing kind of baby. I didn't think she was going to die, so I was shocked when she did. The rhyme led to her death. The word "dead" was orbiting the poem the minute I wrote that her flaw was "dread."

A friend of mine asked me to read that poem at her wedding and I had to convince her otherwise!

AK: In terms of form, some of your pieces are prose poems, to the extent that they're in blocks of text without poetic line breaks. Others are laid out so as to be more readily identified, visually, as poetry. Hearing you read the different kinds of work, however, the distinction is less obvious. Your prose poetry has all the sonic virtues of more conventionally composed free verse, including rhythmic patterning. Could you talk a little about how and when you elect to write in the more compressed prose poetry form, and when in the forms with line breaks?

MH: I think my ear is the same when I'm writing prose poems and lineated poems, but when I write lineated poems I'm really trying to utilize the extra possibilities of the line break. I don't like to read line breaks out loud, though. The line breaks are for the silent reader. Recently I've written a lot of poems about hybrids (Robo-Boy and catgoats and ship figureheads in *Modern Life*) and now a series about mermaids. They seem to naturally want to be written about in a hybrid form.

AK: Speaking of hybrids, you've been involved in several projects that pair poetry with music—notably Philip Glass's—and with photographs. You have the first animation of a poem I'm aware of, and you've done poetry in response to art. And you recently completed a project involving selective erasure of a book about Charles Lamb, to create a new and very different book. Can you tell us more about some of these undertakings, and how they enrich and are enriched by your poetry?

MH: I couldn't have predicted that I would have the opportunity or even desire to collaborate with these various talented people and groups— Elizabeth Zechel on my children's story *The Little General and the Giant Snowflake*, Amy Jean Porter on the illustrated erasure *Of Lamb*, and Eric Moe, who made two choral pieces out of my poems for the Volti choir, and the Miro Quartet. I think I've been experimenting with form through collaboration. How can one's work not be transformed by listening to Philip Glass's String Quartet No. 5?

I recently worked with Adam Shecter on a poster project for a poster collaborative called "2-Up" in which we took a poem I wrote about a constellation called the Suicide Fox—essentially a faux star pattern created by the government to prevent suicide—and Adam transformed it into an iconic almost loony-tunes-like character.

The posters are double-sided and I loved that we came up with the second side just saying "ARE YOU OKAY?" because that really sums up what I want people to ask one another. Also recently Paul Tunis, a writer and cartoonist, took a poem of mine and made that into a graphic poem. The poem (which I've been working on for years during the U.S. Open) always lacked something, and in his illustration, he grounded and complicated the poem perfectly.

Sometimes you find out, out of the blue, that someone has collaborated with your work. Ani Simon-Kennedy made an amazing short inspired by "The Straightforward Mermaid" and it arrived whole in my inbox one day! I couldn't believe it.

AK: Looking over the list of those who have read here in Katonah over the years, can you see any who have been a notable influence for you?

MH: Well, it's such a list! It might be easier to say who hasn't influenced me on this list! Sophie Cabot Black was one of my undergraduate thesis evaluators. I love Lucie Brock-Broido's insanely embroidered work and Donald Justice's odes (he used to be a customer of mine back when I worked at a used bookstore in Iowa City). "Instead of You" by Stephen Dunn was one of the first poems I chose to memorize. I took a class with Marie Ponsot at the 92nd St. Y in a space that was, by day, a kindergarten. You see, I could keep going …

• ● •

PAUL MULDOON

• ● •

Born in County Armagh, Northern Ireland, Paul Muldoon worked in radio and television for the BBC from 1973 to 1986. A protégé and friend of Nobel Prize winner Seamus Heaney, Muldoon published his first book in the early Seventies and has never let up since. While his dazzlingly allusive and casually learned poems may not yield easily to a first reading, their teasing music and sly wit promise to reward a deeper acquaintance.

Since 1987 Muldoon has taught in the U.S., with frequent trips back to Ireland. At Princeton University he is professor of Humanities and Founding Chair of the Lewis Center for the Arts. Among many honors, his over thirty collections of poetry have garnered a Pulitzer Prize and the T.S. Eliot Prize; he is also a Fellow of both the Royal Society of Literature and the American Academy of Arts and Sciences. In a review of his *Selected Poems, 1968-2014*, the *New York Times* called his poetry "allusive, riddling, satirical, strange. . . . His poems set trapdoors—emotional, metrical, intellectual—into which you can fall for miles. . . . You may land with a thunk back in County Armagh, in Northern Ireland, on the farm where he was born. He will have dropped you there (he is poetry editor of *The New Yorker*) from a dizzying urban height."

KPS READING: NOVEMBER 2016

Andrew Kuhn: You are a prodigiously prolific poet who shows no signs of flagging. Your collected poems of 1968 to 1998 would have topped five hundred pages if your publisher hadn't laid them out end to end, with a new poem starting up a couple of spaces below where the previous one left off.

Since then you haven't slowed down. Your most recent collection of poetry, titled *One Thousand Things Worth Knowing* (Farrar, Straus and Giroux, 2016), contains at least that many, and finishes with a wild jalopy (or rather chariot) ride in "Dirty Data," a sort of surreal re-engineering of Ben Hur as an Irish political epic playing out in a mythic and/or kitschy American West.

Do you go through long fallow periods, and then, when inspiration strikes, write at white hot speed? Or do you pretty much write every day, no matter how you happen to be feeling?

Paul Muldoon: I write something every day. It might be a line of a poem. It might be a line of a song. It might be a sentence of a lecture. It might be a response to a question. Each takes a long time. I have no facility with language. I work hard at every sentence. Including this one. I'm still working on it!

AK: Your poems come at the reader thick and fast, so to speak, and particularly for an American it can be hard to keep up. Partly it's a matter of what my middle school English teacher used to call frames of reference, the nomenclature and geographic knowledge and historical markers a writer and his readers may share, or not.

But frames of reference sounds too brittle and rigid to apply here—the sensation is more like having successive nets and webs of reference cast before and over one. There's a willingness in the poems to spin out connections that extend very far and wide, and may at times appear gossamer thin, and yet as a succession of images with rhetorical momentum, the argument of the poem, if one can call it that, seems nonetheless plausible or compelling.

Can you say a little about how "Dirty Data" came to be? And why is it called "Dirty Data"?

PM: According to Wikipedia, the term "Dirty Data" refers to inaccurate, incomplete or erroneous data, especially in a computer system or database. In reference to databases, this is data that contain errors. Unclean data can contain such mistakes as spelling or punctuation errors, incorrect data associated with a field, incomplete or outdated data, or even data that has been duplicated in the database. It can be cleaned through a process known as "data cleansing." I find this idea fascinating, frankly, as it seems to be of a piece with how we conduct ourselves in the world. In terms of Northern Ireland, which is really the "subject" of this poem, it refers specifically to the impossibility of knowing what's going on behind the scenes. What's behind the scenes is the scene itself. That poem is about Bloody Sunday, one of the gravest miscalculations by both sides in the history of the "Troubles."

AK: Formally, your poems seem to echo or evoke specific forms rather than to follow or enact them. Fourteen-line poems with end-rhymes (if you look for them) don't immediately bring to mind sonnets because the line lengths vary so, and the iambs, when they appear, decline to march in formation. Yet your consistency in seeding your poems with rhyme (and off-rhyme, slant-rhyme, third-cousin rhyme) is striking. Can you say a little about the part that rhyme plays for you in composition?

PM: Rhyme is an element of almost everything we do. There's scarcely a sound made that's not echoed. Rhyming is something we hear and see everywhere we listen and look. It's thought to be something artificial. It's the most natural thing in the world. You see that hill? Then that one?

AK: *Madoc: A Mystery* (Farrrar, Straus and Giroux, 1990) appeared a long time ago already—soon after you fetched up in America. The internet was little more than a gleam in some Defense Department researchers' eyes, so these poems' associative reach owed nothing to the experience of surfing the web. But they certainly brought together diverse and disparate elements in a sometimes mysterious way.

You've spoken elsewhere about an interest in and a respect for Freud, to the extent that he made us more aware of an unconscious. Madoc seems to enact the unconscious in a very bold manner. For the unconscious, nothing is incongruous. St. Augustine (in the poem "[AUGUSTINE]") might well concern himself with the problems that the weightily named hamlet of Carthage, New York, was having with the Seneca tribe in 1799. And why shouldn't the Lake Poet Robert Southey get directions to an ale-house, in that same sad, muck-streeted burg, from Alexander the Great's fabled horse, Bucephalus?

Do you think that your having just then broken out of Ulster, indeed of Europe—to whatever extent you might have experienced that move as a breakout—could have contributed to a kind of manic syncretism in these poems? Or was this just a natural extension of the direction you'd been moving in all along?

PM: I do wish sometimes I'd gone a little further down that road. But I'd probably not still be alive. *Madoc* represents an impulse which I have as a matter of course, but which I tend not to follow to the extent I might. I like the idea that all poems should be avant-garde, yet I find much self-identifying avant-gardism terribly boring.

AK: In the world of poetry there have been other displacements with reverberations and aftershocks. Auden was rounded on for leaving Britain when the Nazis were advancing, which you evoke in his own voice in the astonishing series of linked poems, "7, Middagh Street."

Did you experience significant static politically, critically, socially, for abandoning the old sod, to put it melodramatically?

PM: I never left the old sod in any serious way. I took a job offer thirty years ago and, for better or worse, am still here. I was in Ireland two weeks ago. And two weeks before that. I'm still very attached to the place.

AK: I have never encountered a poet post-Shakespeare who has enlarged my vocabulary as rapidly as you have. Without the multiple dictionaries accessible online I would not have known, for example, that a *turnip clamp* is a house-sized mound of turnips; *spraint*, the dung of otters; *firedamp*, explosive methane gas that dangerously accumulates in mines; *thole*, to endure something without complaint, to tolerate. All these appear in a single poem, "Cuthbert and the Otters," subtitled, "In Memory of Seamus Heaney." I hadn't previously heard of St. Cuthbert, nor of his nocturnal dips in the cold Atlantic with the local romp of otters, who reportedly thought highly of him.

Is this recondite vocabulary all at the tip of your own tongue, or do you need some swatting up yourself from time to time? Would Seamus Heaney himself have made it all the way through "Cuthbert" without recourse to any outside reference, do you think?

PM: I use only what I think is the right word at the right time and in the right place. Seamus had a big vocabulary and would have had no trouble with this poem. But no one need have trouble with it. If one doesn't recognize a word, one should look it up. There's no shame in that. Had Seamus not recognized a usage he'd have looked it up. It's pretty basic.

AK: Looking at the collected terms, in "Cuthbert" for example, it appears that most of them are of the earth, referring to animals and artifacts that attach to a specific geography, and a line of Scottish and Norman and Middle English linguistic descent, and a way of life that is largely past. When you arrived in the U.S., you have said, you figured you weren't going to be writing any more poems about pig killers. But on the occasion of your return to Ireland for this funeral, you evoke this largely lost world. Is that partly by way of homage, an honoring of roots that nourished both Seamus Heaney and you?

PM: I'm sure that's right. But pig-killing isn't something that's stopped. It's still big business. In fact, I think my next book may be devoted to pig-killing.

AK: Can't wait.

Your collection of essays is entitled *The End of the Poem*—a title involving some misdirection, to the extent that it evokes a gloomy "end of poetry" idea, whereas for the most part in these essays "end" seems to be taken to mean "purpose" or "intention." You enact bold and intimate readings of particular poems and poets, and don't hesitate to deploy biographical information in an effort to develop insight into the sources and meanings of specific choices, elisions, revisions, suppressions the poet makes.

Do you ever subject your own work to this kind of analysis? Would you want to read it if someone else did?

PM: I'd like to think that my own poems would withstand the kind of scrutiny I give the poems in *The End of the Poem*. They're certainly constructed with that level of scrutiny in mind. Any work of art should be able to withstand such intense focus. If I hadn't been into that all along I wouldn't ever have got into the business. And, of course, I believe absolutely that the poem itself knows more than I do.

AK: Before Bob Dylan was awarded the Nobel Prize in Literature, I believe you were far and away the most successful poet who is or has ever been also a bona fide rocker. You wrote songs for and with Warren Zevon and the band Rackett, with whom you play rhythm guitar; you also published a collection of thirty rock song lyrics, *Word on the Street*.

What do you think of Dylan's lyrics as poetry? Or as lyrics, for that matter? Did he have any influence on you as a poet?

PM: I'm pretty sure popular song has been part of the back of the mind for many poets for at least one hundred years. Or is it one thousand years? In the twentieth century, Eliot was deeply influenced by that tradition. The number of allusions to popular song in "The Waste Land" is remarkable by any standards. We think of that poem as being primarily a collage; it's at least as useful to think of it as a very mixed chorus.

The poet who was a bona fide rocker was not me, by the way. I'm just an amateur, a poseur. The real rocker would be Leonard Cohen (of recent memory) or Paul Simon. In that regard, it doesn't matter to me if something is a song or a poem or, indeed, neither. All that matters is whether or not they're any good at what they're setting out to do. That's something we can figure out pretty quickly.

· ● ·

AIMEE NEZHUKUMATATHIL

• • •

Aimee Nezhukumatathil, poetry editor of *Orion* magazine, is author of three acclaimed poetry collections: *Lucky Fish* (2011); *At The Drive-In Volcano* (2007), winner of the Balcones Prize; and *Miracle Fruit* (2003). She is currently Professor of English at State University of New York-Fredonia (what she likes to call "berry country"), where she teaches creative writing and environmental literature. Due out in 2018 is a collection of illustrated nature essays, *World of Wonder*. Ms. Nezhukumatathil's poems have appeared in the *Best American Poetry* series, *American Poetry Review*, *New England Review*, *Poetry*, *Ploughshares*, and *Tin House*.

Terrance Hayes wrote this about the collection *Lucky Fish*: "A farmer is devoured by a flower in one of the many beguiling poems of *Lucky Fish*. This is the sensation I often had reading Aimee Nezhukumatathil's wonderful new collection—that of being immersed in a limber intelligence. Rooted in the terrains of culture, place, and parenthood, and buoyed by inventive language that is joyous and sincere, *Lucky Fish* is a book of copious heart and imagination. How wonderful to watch a writer who was already among the best young poets get even better!"

KPS READING: OCTOBER 2011

Andrew Kuhn: Your poems have a terrific range of reference in them, and all kinds of out-of-the-way words and facts—like "dinoflagellates" and "monkey spiders." Yet your voice in the poems is very direct, unpretentious, conversational. It's sort of like listening to a very excited friend who's high on words.

Aimee Nezhukumatathil: Thanks. With a very few exceptions, the voice in my poems is quite similar to my own speaking voice and so I'm sure you wouldn't be surprised to know that my pleasure reading usually involves science and nature books, field guides, natural history collections, and so on. So I suppose some of the vibrant language from those types of texts sometimes invades my daily speech. My husband is so used to me talking about a rare jellyfish for example in one sentence and the next thing out of my mouth is about fixing a porch light, but I can see how it can be a tad jarring if you've newly met me.

AK: You grew up in Chicago, and your accent is American, but there are other pieces to your background that have had an influence on your life and your approach to language. Can you tell me a little about your name?

AN: It's my maiden name—my father's—who is from Kerala, in south India. Since my parents had two girls, I couldn't bear to change my name and my husband thankfully never wanted me to change my name either. In fact, he said he would be "disappointed" if I did change it . . .

You know, another piece to my development in language and in writing is that I came to poetry relatively late compared to most of my peers. I never knew there were living poets until my junior year of college. I started out, as many children of doctors do, as pre-med, majoring in chemistry. I'm glad I switched to English, but I still have a deep love of the language of the sciences, the musicality of the names of flora and fauna . . . Even various elements and molecules have a music to their names, so I think that might hopefully carry over into my writing.

AK: You're young—thirty-ish?—and already you have three books out, a bunch of awards, and you're a professor. You may have come to poetry later than some of your peers, but it seems you got going pretty fast.

AN: Well, I'm actually 36. I've been deeply blessed to have a great mentor at Ohio State—the late David Citino. And the writing community of Madison, Wisconsin, where I was on a poetry fellowship for a year after grad school, gave me crucial support just as I was assembling what would later become my first book of poems. I always felt my peers in grad school were much better read than me, and so much of my poetry education has been reading and reading, trying to fill in the blanks of what I wasn't exposed to in high school and early college. But I've always loved to read and that, above all else, has been key to my development as a writer. I'm always bewildered when I encounter a student who wants to be a writer, but doesn't want to read.

AK: Your life has changed a good deal in a few years, I understand—marriage, two kids. Has that affected the way you approach writing, and your subject matter?

AN: Well the obvious answer is that the new developments in my family—I have a four-year-old who just started preschool this week, and a fifteen-month-old—have forced me to be more efficient in smaller bursts of time. But my husband is also a writer and I try to make it a priority for both of us to squeeze in some writing during the week—we both are very present in our sons' lives—I think it would be too easy to be resentful or be daydreaming I was somewhere else if I didn't have that outlet.

As for how it's affected my subject matter, I'd best leave that to others, but I feel like there is a deeper sense of celebration and gratitude for the small things in life, perhaps more of a sense of urgency now in my newer work.

AK: You're on the road a lot. Is that draining, or do you get a certain kind of energy from meeting your readers?

AN: Both. But whatever tiredness I feel is assuaged by the dynamics of being a visiting writer or a workshop leader in both high schools and universities all over the country. I actually do love readings very much—so much of your time as a writer is spent alone in a room, and readings and workshops are a way to connect and have a conversation with an audience and get out of my own headspace, so to speak. I love the immediacy of that connection, too.

AK: Looking at the list of our past readers, do any stand out as having influenced your development as a poet?

AN: Sharon Olds and Dorianne Laux are two that spring to mind when I think of those early heady days spent reading and sitting on the floor of the Ohio State library—two women who wrote about the body and being a woman in such honest and visceral ways—and though I think my poems are very different, I think reading their books gave me a sense of permission to write about the body, of motherhood, and to not be scared of having a sense of vulnerability on the page, too.

AK: What have you been working on lately? Do you plan to share some recent work at the reading?

AN: Right now I am working a bit more on lyric nature essays, so I won't read those during my visit, but new poems are always brewing at any given time in my little blue office. I just finished a summer exchange of poems via post mail with a dear friend, the poet Ross Gay, whose own writing I adore so much, so I am also working on revisions of those early drafts. So I might try out one or another of those—you'll just have to see!

· ● ·

D. NURKSE

• ● •

D. Nurkse a/k/a Dennis Nurkse, has served as Poet Laureate of Brook-
lyn, as befits a man with a cosmopolitan background. His artist mother
and diplomat Estonian father came to the U.S. to escape the Nazis, and
Nurkse partly grew up in Europe. As a poet, he is strikingly down-
to-earth; many of his poems evoke various and specifically rendered
worlds of work (urban, American) in vivid and unsentimental ways.
The breadth of Nurkse's sympathies can be glimpsed in the places he
has taught, from Sarah Lawrence to the Riker's Island Correctional
Facility in New York. He has written about human rights, and served
on the board of directors of Amnesty International, USA.

Nurkse's ten collections include *A Night In Brooklyn* (2012), *The
Border Kingdom* (2008), *The Fall* (2003), and *The Rules of Paradise*
(2001). He has won awards and fellowships from the Guggenheim
Foundation, the National Endowment for the Arts, the American
Academy of Arts and Letters, the Poetry Foundation and the Tanne
Foundation. His work has been widely translated. A *New Yorker* critic
wrote about *Voices Over Water*: "These poems work both as discrete,
individually imagined lyrics and also as chapters in an ongoing narra-
tive of genuinely engaging lives. . . . A high proportion of the poems
are gems of gravid simplicity, and Nurkse's rhetorical periods can be
breathtaking."

KPS READING: NOVEMBER 2012

Andrew Kuhn: Your tenth book of poetry is named *A Night in Brooklyn* (Alfred A. Knopf, 2012). The title poem brings together sexual love, the brute and unlovely physical realities of the city, and the ceaseless creative and destructive activity of imagination in an off-hand, surreal way.

A Night in Brooklyn

We undid a button,
turned out the light,
and in that narrow bed
we built the great city—
water towers, cisterns,
hot asphalt roofs, parks,
septic tanks, arterial roads,
Canarsie, the intricate channels,
the seacoast, underwater mountains,
bluffs, islands, the next continent,
using only the palms of our hands
and the tips of our tongues, next
we made darkness itself, by then
it was time for dawn
and we closed our eyes
and counted to ourselves
until the sun rose
and we had to take it all to pieces
for there could be only one Brooklyn.

The end of the poem has a kind of rueful humor to it, partly because already in this short poem you've given us a lot of Brooklyns. But you also seem to suggest that the imaginative fervor of lovers and poets does have to yield at dawn to the enormity of the actual city. Oh well! It's a kind of creation myth. Can you say a little about the origins of the poem, and how it developed?

D. Nurkse: Thanks, Andrew. A theme of *A Night in Brooklyn* is how we make up stories, believe them, and live in them as if they were worlds. But this poem is playful—it's giving the sexual act the power to transform everything around it; which, of course, it has, but only to the participants. This poem also fools around with the tradition of the aubade and the alba, the troubadour and classical poems of lovers confronting dawn.

AK: Brooklyn means a lot of things to a lot of people by now, and it seems to be always changing. (I'm guessing that at least a third of the audience who will turn out for your reading will be former Brooklyn residents, like me). What are some of the compelling elements of Brooklyn for you as a place to live, and as a place for the imagination to take hold?

DN: Brooklyn throughout my life has been a place of vastness and wildness. I remember immense ruined factories; neighborhoods where diners sold ake ake, saltfish, cowsfoot soup, comfort food from West Africa; neighborhoods where you would hear Malayalam, Quechua, Ladino. I once accompanied a great Irish poet who read in Gaelic in Irish Brooklyn. I remember bars where ex-guerrillas spoke of fighting the Bloody Black and Tans.

I love the sea and the mountains. Brooklyn really had the same sense of being beyond measure. I remember teaching poetry to Orthodox Jewish children. One young girl came up with the line "red is the color of dying in your sleep." The parents were startled, halted the workshop, and consulted a rabbi as to whether the exploration of poetry was safe or psychically dangerous. The rabbi felt that confronting the depths was entirely healthy and the parents invited me back.

AK: You write about various trades—some of them long since vanished from Brooklyn, I imagine—with sensuous, even loving specificity. I take it you've done some work that wasn't teaching poetry? You don't romanticize labor, you include the tedium and the occasional, sudden danger, but there seems to be a way that you're quietly honoring the act of work, if that's not too gushy.

Excelsior Fashion Products, Easter

They pay us time and a half
and don't dare catch us
drinking: we don't insist,
don't pass a bottle, but each sips
a private pint, all sitting
in the narrow room with our backs
to the center, each facing
his work—router, stain tray,
buffing wheel, drill press—
and with that sweet taste echoing
in our bones, we watch our hands
make what they always made
—rosewood handles—but now
we smile in delighted surprise
and Marchesi brings envelopes
that record a full day's work
though it's still noon,
processions still fill the streets,
choirs, loudspeakers bellowing
Hallelujah: and we change
into our finest clothes in the locker room,
admiring each other's hat brims, passing bottles
freely until all are empty, and at last
we separate in the brilliant street, each
in the direction of a different tolling bell.

[From *The Rules of Paradise*, 2001]

How have your experiences working for a living affected your choice of materials and your approach to the craft of writing?

DN: I'm grateful that earning my living in different ways—blue-collar work for many years—gave me a bye from the dependencies and politics of academia. I'm equally grateful that academia was there to shelter me later in life. I was given insight into different classes and sets of expectations. Carpentry and construction left me fascinated with processes, with the textures of unfinished work before the final coat which is designed to domesticate labor and make it invisible.

AK: Sometimes the "making" in your poems is very specific and concrete, as in "Making Shelves." Whatever else they might be, these are real shelves—even though the making of them summons forth a dead man.

Making Shelves

In that lit window in Bushwick
halfway through the hardest winter
I cut plexiglass on a table saw,
coaxing the chalked taped pane
into the absence of the blade,
working to such fine tolerance
the kerf abolished the soft-lead line.
I felt your eyes play over me
but did not turn—dead people
were not allowed in those huge factories.
I bargained: when the bell rang
I would drink with you on Throop
under the El, quick pint of Night Train
but you said no. Blood jumped

from my little finger, power
snapped off, voices summoned me
by name, but I waved them back
and knelt to rule the next line.

[From *A Night in Brooklyn*, 2012]

AK: But in "Nights on the Peninsula" (as in "A Night in Brooklyn") the making is profligate and protean, beyond god-like, surreal.

Nights on the Peninsula

We could not separate ourselves from our endless making.
We were always fabricating time, God, paradise,
the bell-shaped lupines, the rough-grained elm
and smooth beech. We made the night sky from a rusty hinge,
the sea from a sigh and a bead of sweat. We made love
long before dawn. We constantly modified each other,
adding a leer to the other's face, or a smirk, even in sleep.
What kind of a tool-maker invents eternity and exile

and makes them race, like a child with the index and middle finger?
Even in dreams we bore the burden of waking, we called it suffering.
Even in a trance we had maps and blueprints. In the deepest dream
we received the gift of death—it rained on that peninsula.
The wind passed like a sponge over the gambrel roofs.
The leaves showed a blank side, veined like a cresting wave.
We were almost home, we thought. We had never seen this world
but we sensed it, like a cat's breath against our wrists:
we were married, the bees loved us, the ocean might relent,
the child muttered over a handful of dust and spit.

[From *A Night in Brooklyn*, 2012]

Both "Making Shelves" and "Nights on the Peninsula," though, are characterized by a kind of dread. Is there something anxious-making about the making and the makers in these poems?

DN: As you point out, these poems have different agendas. In "Making Shelves" there's a little elegy to a vanished world of labor; the factory is trespassed on by the dead precursor. In "Nights on the Peninsula" I'm thinking of the obsessive power of consciousness, the automatism of the mind, which reflexively arranges clues into chains of meaning—how the psyche can't help identifying, projecting, animating.

AK: When people talk about poets in New York, especially since World War Two, the names of the New York School come up—John Ashbery, Frank O'Hara and Kenneth Koch in the first wave, for example, then Ron Padgett, Ted Berrigan, Anne Waldman in the Sixties. They seem to have made pretty tight and collaborative groups. A lot of them were also active in or inspired by the visual arts. Has there been any sort of analogous movement or school or gang of poets coming out of Brooklyn more recently? Has there been that sort of cross-pollination between poets and artists, or poets and musicians?

DN: There are really many schools blooming at once. We're pluralistic. People (though not me) meet on the web instead of the local bar. Though places like Barbès and Sistas' Place and the Central Brooklyn

Jazz Festival and any amount of coffeehouses continue to be hubs of culture. I have my own friends in the jazz community. The visual arts are flourishing wildly.

AK: Poets associated with New York didn't necessarily come from there—the New York School could almost have been the Tulsa School, since Ashbery and Berrigan and Joe Brainard all came from there originally. (How much of Tulsa shines through their poetry is a subject for somebody's dissertation, maybe). Your parents were European, and what little I know of your upbringing sounds international and peripatetic. Was English your mother tongue? Where do you feel that you are from? How have your travels influenced your experience of Brooklyn, and your writing?

DN: Yes, my family came here from Europe as the Nazis were coming to power, and we moved back to Europe briefly in the early sixties. My family members got by in many languages, but English was my first language. That's probably an affinity to Brooklyn: living there is like traveling, being everywhere and nowhere. My current neighborhood is a place of immigrants, and I like their outlook. They take nothing for granted.

AK: How did you get to be the poet laureate of Brooklyn, what were your duties, and what should an aspiring future poet laureate of Brooklyn be doing to enhance his or her chances of ascending to that post?

DN: I was nominated for the position and appointed by a panel. I had no fixed duties. I did a lot of workshops in inner-city neighborhoods, schools, literacy centers, and libraries—in Bed-Stuy, East Flatbush, Canarsie, Gerritsen Beach; places other than the traditional cultural meccas in Williamsburg, Brooklyn Heights, and Park Slope. An aspiring poet laureate is probably in the wrong field; poetry is a lovely thing but you can't do it for political gain. That has to be, at best, an afterthought.

AK: You write love poetry, unapologetically, un-ironically even, and it's sexy and moving and sometimes even romantic. But even in a love poem you can brutalize the reader with a sudden turn.

A Marriage in the Dolomites

We communicated by cheeses,
unwrapping them gingerly,
parting the crust with a fork,
tasting dew, must, salt,
raising an eyebrow,

or we let chianti talk for us,
rolling it in the glass,
staring—it was dark and shiny
as the pupil, and stared back—
or we undressed each other;

we took long walks hand in hand
in the vineyards, the pastures,
resenting each other bitterly
for our happiness that excluded us
as surely as the world did,
mountain after mountain.

[*Poetry*, June 2009]

AK: That "resenting each other bitterly" comes as a shock; the perversity of "for our happiness that excluded us" is so opaque and complete that it seems to exclude even the possibility of sustained connection or love or even contentment. The couple in the poem never speaks a word. Is that the problem, or a failed attempt at a solution?

DN: I don't know—your interpretation is valid, but I read this poem more lightly. I think it's a little tongue-in-cheek: two people overwhelmed by the happiness they've brought each other. I think happiness is much more dangerous than suffering; that's why people work so hard to make themselves and others unhappy. These two may be speechless in front of each other, but they tell their story in "couple" pronouns, and the happiness that they feel excluding them (does the world really?) remains "ours."

AK: "Searchers" is a terrifically haunting poem that evokes 9/11, very obliquely at first, then in a devastating way.

Searchers

We gave our dogs a button to sniff,
or a tissue, and they bounded off
confident in their training,
in the power of their senses
to re-create the body,

but after eighteen hours in rubble
where even steel was pulverized
they curled on themselves
and stared up at us
and in their soft huge eyes
we saw mirrored the longing for death:

then we had to beg a stranger
to be a victim and crouch
behind a girder, and let the dogs
discover him and tug him
proudly, with suppressed yaps,
back to Command and the rows
of empty triage tables.

But who will hide from us?
Who will keep digging for us
here in the cloud of ashes?

[From *Burnt Island*, 2005]

AK: The searchers seem to dematerialize and become the vanished ones they've been vainly searching for. Were you living in New York in September 2001? What sort of impact did it have on your life and work?

DN: Thanks, Andrew. I was not just in New York in September 2001, but downtown. I saw more than I wanted to. The event was horrible in itself; its transformation into an iconic spectacle was profoundly chilling. The reactions of regular citizens, as opposed to ideologues, were very moving. People helped each other for a few days as never before or since. I lived in a fireman's neighborhood and knew people who could name a hundred people they lost on that day. It's deeply offensive to something bedrock in human nature that there were no dead bodies to bury, as there were no wounded to tend to. And I'll never forgive the City for saying the air was fine and not requiring masks for rescue workers. They breathed titanium, PCBs, and asbestos.

AK: The Katonah Poetry Series has brought leading poets to read at the Katonah Village Library since 1967. Looking over our list of past readers, are there any who have had an influence on your development as a poet?

DN: There are friends and quite a few colleagues in that list. Poets as different as Stephen Dunn and Muriel Rukeyser were kind to me when I was isolated, as I was for much of my life—I didn't take the MFA train. If this interview were spoken and not written, I'd propose concluding with a moment of silence for Paul Violi, a superb poet who died last year.

• • •

KATHLEEN OSSIP

• ● •

Kathleen Ossip's poems have appeared in *Poetry*, *The Paris Review*, *Poetry Review*, *The Washington Post*, and *Best American Poetry*. Her collection, *The Do-Over* (2015), was a *New York Times* Editor's Choice. Derek Walcott selected *The Search Engine* for the American Poetry Review/Honickman First Book Prize. Both *Publisher's Weekly* and NPR picked *The Cold War* as one of their best poetry books for the year 2011. Ossip has also published *Cinephrastics*, a chapbook of movie poems. *Laurus* magazine noted that this "ironic, intimate meditation on observation. . . . throw[s] a sly, fresh, and most of all gentle blow at the common notion that those who critique art do so because they can't create it." A founding editor of the poetry review website *SCOUT*, Ossip teaches at the New School.

In *The New York Times*, Stephen Burt observed about *The Do-Over*, "Ossip writes to remember the dead . . . to face her own death without panic, if she can; to help us face ours; and to show how an aggressively up-to-date vocabulary—one that would make a lesser writer sound jaded, or bored, or distracted by pings from her iPhone—can fit the most serious of poetic concerns."

KPS READING: SEPTEMBER 2016

Andrew Kuhn: You have written elegies, sonnets, rants, odes, thumbnail biographies, prose poems, acrostics, lyrics ultra-compressed and expansive, "true" flash fictions, and even a full-scale short story in prose—and this all just in your much-celebrated, third full-scale collection of poetry, *The Do-Over*, published in 2015. You have taken on the Cold War, pop icons, death with a capital D, and love, and desire, and being a mother. You are such a protean poet it's hard to know where to begin.

Not quite at random, let's start with "On Beauty." It is reproduced in full below.

On Beauty

Firstly, you are beautiful,
moonfaced brothers and sisters.

But after that, what
is not open to question?

To pick up the torn wing
and paperclip it onto the angel

is a distortion rapidly done.
Distortion is beautiful,

and loud hearty laughter
as of the gods.

Beauty moves upwards from the leaf,
downwards from the root.

Beauty is quietly
born from boredom

into fabulousness or plainness.
Don't ask whether it exists.

It's a redundancy to say real.
Beauty is truth? Don't ask.

Ask for inner resources unlimited.
Ask for a goldfinch feather

in a balsawood box.
Look not at what is loved

but what stimulates and soothes.
Brothers and sisters,

are words beautiful or ugly
because we mean them

so very deeply?

[From *The Do-Over*, 2015]

Stunning poem. A lot of poets nowadays would run screaming for the exits rather than take on an abstract, classic subject like "Beauty," especially with the prefix "On", which almost seems to defiantly double down on the ambition. "Thanks, Aristotle—I'll take it from here."

Can you say a little about how you came to write this poem? Was there anything in particular in your reading or your life at the time that you can recall having sparked or formed the germ of it?

Kathleen Ossip: Yes, I remember exactly what made me interested in taking on that big abstract subject. It wasn't Aristotle but Francis Bacon. I was visiting my parents and they had a volume of his collected essays, and I started reading it. They all have titles like "Of Truth," "Of Death," "Of Adversity," etc. I always tell my students to go in fear of big abstract nouns, but I liked Bacon's ambition and his questioning but argument-driven approach.

I like trying to figure things out, and I wondered if you could do something similar in a poem without being unbearably preachy or dull. I wrote "On Beauty" and "On Sadness," which is in *The Do-Over*, as companions. Since then I've written "On Giving Birth" and I'm currently working on "On Boredom."

AK: The assurance, even the bravura, of your opening is characteristic of much of your work, I think.

> Firstly, you are beautiful,
> moonfaced brothers and sisters.
>
> But after that, what
> is not open to question?

It's not obvious that moonfaced brothers and sisters would be beautiful, let alone so beautiful that it would not be open to question. But you sell us on this notion, even while rhetorically undercutting it immediately, orienting us that even the most emphatic statements to follow may turn out to be standing on thin air. You go on:

> To pick up the torn wing
> and paperclip it onto the angel
>
> is a distortion rapidly done.
> Distortion is beautiful,
>
> and loud hearty laughter
> as of the gods.

Already we're in trouble—way over our heads. The magisterial assertions are coming so thick and fast we don't know what to make of them, really. And yet we want to believe. We believe!

Of course, we think, it must be true, for example, that to pick up a torn wing and to paperclip it onto an angel is a distortion. And naturally, such an operation, with the wing and the paperclip, would be rapidly done. . . Once you have posited angels and paperclips in the same frame, you are free to describe their interaction according to the natural laws of the universe you have conjured, at least for the moment.

How important has it been for you as a writer to establish early and often the degrees of freedom you are claiming in a given piece, a given collection?

KO: I'm not sure that establishing my freedom is a conscious process, but freedom is very important to me, and one reason I like writing poems is that they're an utterly free space, one of a very few I can think of. That's why writing poems is a political act.

AK: In another poem you confide, "Facts never did anything for us." This past week in *The New York Times* Dwight Garner interviewed Langdon Hammer about his biography of James Merrill, who—as I'm sure you and our readers know—was fascinated by the Ouija board and turned his engagement with it into a celebrated book-length poem.

Merrill was apparently also friends with and greatly admired Elizabeth Bishop (Hammer's next biographical subject). Hammer, however, noted that Bishop was not crazy about Merrill's Ouija poem, telling him "not so delicately that it just doesn't make sense." Hammer goes on, "Like a biographer, Bishop cared about facts (or at least pretended to)."

Would you place yourself more in the Merrill camp, or the Bishop camp? Or do you object to such oppositions as unwarranted restrictions on one's range of motion as a poet?

KO: As a reader, Bishop means more to me than Merrill; I can't quite get beyond the nonchalant background tone of privilege in Merrill's work, though this is only a personal preference—my limitation, not Merrill's. (And it's there in Bishop too, of course, much muted.) For a long time after I read Bishop in graduate school, I felt that she knew the shape of a poem more intimately and more surely than anyone else. By shape, I don't mean only form, but progression, pace, what to put in overtly, what to gesture at, what to leave out, when to use facts and when to use flights of fancy, and much more. I've modeled several poems very closely on some of hers.

I think when I wrote "Facts never did anything for us," I meant that I don't find facts very useful when deciding "how to live and what to do." This is partly because when you look closely at a "fact" you tend to notice how quickly they dissolve into, at best, partial facts.

But on the issue of facts in poems, I believe facts are grist as much as anything else: lies, dreams, fantasies, imagining…

AK: Twice in this short poem, "On Beauty," you address your readers as "brothers and sisters." Are you aware of any impulse in yourself to preach a sermon, to get an amen? Much of the poem is in the imperative mode—carrying an unspoken but unmistakable "You should" if not "Thou shalt." You borrow other preacherly rhetorical tropes besides the brothers-and-sisters one: "Look not," for instance. Who says that? And, of course, you do mention an angel . . .

You've spoken elsewhere about being raised Catholic, which I imagine must have involved regular exposure to sermons if not also sermonizing. Do you think hearing such cadences and modes of address has affected the development of your poetry?

KO: Guilty! I'm very prone to the didactic, I'm sure, sometimes to a fault. I try to rein it in, but I figure it's better to channel it into poems than in face-to-face interactions. And yes, my Catholic background, which included Catholic school, is an influence.

AK: Another startling assertion is this:

> Beauty is quietly
> born from boredom
>
> into fabulousness or plainness.

This is a provocative, original, weird aphorism. We can picture the bored beauty, or the bored artist finally goaded by her own boredom to create a thing of beauty. You mentioned just now you've returned to boredom as a topic . . . What role does boredom play in your own creative process?

KO: A big role. I'm easily over-stimulated and I find it impossible to feel creative when I get in that state. Cultivating a boring (or soothing) environment makes me fill it with my own daydreams and imaginings and interior language.

AK: In this take, beauty is not static—it has a career, developing into either fabulousness or plainness. (Both would seem to be a comedown from the original ideal or idealized state). So, far from being "a joy forever," for instance, beauty is subject to time, like the rest of us.

Do you set out with the intention of frankly trying to make something beautiful, when you make a poem? Are you mistrustful of that impulse at all, or feel any pressure to hide it under a bushel?

KO: I always set out trying to make something beautiful. For me, that's part of the definition of a poem.

But beauty isn't limited to Keats-ian beauty (or fill in whatever name you like). I teach poetry workshops at The New School, where my students are often a mix of undergraduates and older continuing education students. One day, one undergraduate brought in a terrific poem he'd written using environmental text, language he found around him on the city streets, which included the line "Think noodles." An older woman student said, in response, with a dissatisfied tone, "When are we going to talk about beauty?" I told her that I thought "Think noodles" was a very beautiful bit of language. And I do, I'm very attracted to that kind of plain, fresh, flat language. That was in my mind when I wrote that "fabulousness or plainness" line.

AK: After developing a rhetoric of great assurance, the turn at the very end of "On Beauty" is disarming. The question seems not to have been asked for effect, but in a spirit of genuine wonder.

> Brothers and sisters,
>
> are words beautiful or ugly
> because we mean them
>
> so very deeply?

Despite the multiple ironies and indirections that came before, this closing registers as a moment of true feeling. There's an admission of a vulnerability in common—an invitation to consider the mystery of the shared passion that we bring to words, and that they bring to us.

The ambit of this interview was more deep than broad; to those readers looking for a more comprehensive survey of your work, I apologize. Will the poems you'll be reading at the library here be consonant with some of what we've been discussing with respect to "On Beauty"? Or have I just perpetrated false advertising?

KO: I appreciate the close reading! I hope to be both consistent and surprising.

AK: Looking at the list of past Katonah Poetry Series readers, do you see any who have been particularly influential for your development as a writer?

KO: What a fantastic, varied group of poets! I'm thrilled to be one of them. As for influences, I've always liked Anne Sexton's belief that "We are all writing the poem of our time." If that's true, we're all influencing each other in all possible ways and in all possible directions, like the physicists tell us.

• ● •

ROBERT PINSKY

• ● •

An extraordinarily accomplished man of letters, with numerous highly praised collections of poetry, works of prose, anthologies and translations to his name, Robert Pinsky served as U.S. Poet Laureate from 1997 to 2000. Honors include an American Academy of Arts and Letters Award, a Guggenheim, two awards from the Poetry Society of America, and the PEN/Voelcker Award for Poetry. His poetry has been collected in *Selected Poems* (2011); *Gulf Music: Poems* (2007); *Jersey Rain* (2000); *The Figured Wheel: New and Collected Poems 1966-1996* (1996), which received the 1997 Lenore Marshall prize and was a Pulitzer Prize nominee; *The Want Bone* (1990); *History of My Heart* (1984); *An Explanation of America* (1980); and *Sadness and Happiness* (1975). His most recent collection is *At the Foundling Hospital* (2016).

Renowned as a teacher, during his term as Poet Laureate Pinsky began the Favorite Poem Project, organizing events at which people would read or recite a favorite poem and say something about what this poem in particular meant to them. The project lives on with three anthologies, many videos on its website, and annual week-long summer institutes for educators led by Pinsky and other poets. The famously difficult-to-impress poet and critic Louise Glück paid him this tribute. "Robert Pinsky has what I think Shakespeare must have had: dexterity combined with worldliness, the magician's dazzling quickness fused with subtle intelligence."

KPS READING: APRIL 2016

Andrew Kuhn: With such an impressive and impressively large body of work, it's hard to know where to begin.

It's conventional to think of the Big Novel (and more parochially the Great American Novel) as the ultimate in literary ambition, but one could argue that when it comes to swinging for the fences (America again) the trajectory of some of your poems soars over any mere narrative project. Some of your poems seem to encompass not just the usual human themes of attachment and disastrous loss, for instance, but the whole laughable, tragic, tenuous place of man in the history of a small planet full of marvels.

"The Hearts" is one astonishing example among many. Anatomy, Enobarbus, Shakespeare, the Buddha, the destruction of the Temple, the seraphim of the Lord, and Lee Andrews and the Hearts circa 1957—all vividly surge and mingle in a hallucinatory flood of 29 incantatory three-line stanzas. You have written much great poetry since "The Hearts" (*The Want Bone*, in which it appeared, came out in 1990). But can you recall how you came to make such a poem, and if you were intentionally staking out a vast territory as the proper domain of poetry (and, in particular, your own)?

Robert Pinsky: In my late teens I responded deeply to a definition of the epic: "a poem containing history." So said Ezra Pound, a terrible man who said many good things. I liked the way "containing" can mean not just "including" but "comprehending, mastering, making sense of" the past.

And as a patriotic American I take "history" to be larger than just the doings of rulers and armies: to include, in the example of "The Hearts," the music of Lee Andrews (recently deceased father of Questlove) along with the Buddha, the Jewish prophets, Antony and Cleopatra: all belonging to whatever heart embraces them, all part of what James Baldwin calls our "birthright" as distinct from our "inheritance."

So, the poem tries to sing about the eccentric, layered inheritance, as part of one person's emotional life.

"Sing" is an important word here, I guess. In relation to your question, the novel, with those perfectly rectangular blocks of print, that concern with property and marriage, is an Industrial Revolution form. Poetry is much older than that, as old as song.

And thank you, Andy, for what you say about the poem. The idea of a wide embrace, and headlong, inclusive music—important to me.

AK: You have not shied away from being not only learned in your poems, but even at times didactic. "Ginza Samba" (*The Figured Wheel*, 1996) introduces us to the inventor of the saxophone but quickly widens, like the air issuing from that instrument's bell:

> . . . its column of vibrating
> Air shaped not in a cylinder but in a cone
> Widening ever outward and bawaah spouting
> Infinitely upward through an upturned
> Swollen golden bell rimmed
> Like a gloxinia flowering
> In Sax's Belgian imagination.

This sonically gorgeous overture quickly quickens to a devilishly complex riff weaving anatomy and history with serious jazz puns:

> And in the unfathomable matrix
> Of mothers and fathers as a genius graven
> Humming into the cells of the body
> Or saved cupped in the resonating grail
> Of memory changed and exchanged
> As in the trading of brasses,
> Pearls and ivory, calicos and slaves,
> Laborers and girls, two
>
> Cousins in a royal family
> Of Niger known as the Birds or Hawks.

The point of view here is transcendent, surpassing the constraints of any individual's history, or even any conventional emotional response to human suffering.

In the belly of a slaveship to the port
Of Baltimore where she is raped
And dies in childbirth, but the infant
Will marry a Seminole and in the next
Chorus of time their child fathers
A great Hawk or Bird, with many followers
Among them this great-grandchild of the Jewish
Manager of a Pushkin estate, blowing

His American breath out into the wiggly
Tune uncurling its triplets and sixteenths . . .

No divinity is invoked, and there is no readily discernible moral to the story you are telling. Yet in its temporal sweep and miraculous connections and tone of passionate praise, the poem has the sacred aura of a foundational myth. (Reminded me a little in its exuberant language and material of the novelist Ishmael Reed, who wrote *Mumbo Jumbo* and *The Free-Lance Pallbearers*.) So . . . Does jazz and its history have a spiritual resonance for you?

RP: Jazz is at the core of my feeling for art. Your comparison to the work of my friend and Berkeley colleague Ishmael— a great compliment. I read both "Ginza Samba" and "The Hearts" on the *PoemJazz* CD with the great pianist Laurence Hobgood.

Jazz, originating with the blues, exemplifies the terrifying, half-way-redeemed story of culture itself: our most truly, uniquely American cultural form, with its musical descendants, grows out of slavery. Another example of "history" as larger than wars, dynasties, elections: the African ancestor of the Russian poet Aleksandr Pushkin, the African ancestor of the American musician Charlie Parker—those ancestors only part of the work and life of those geniuses, one strand of the birthright that is only attainable (returning to Baldwin's terms) through the limiting, inescapable inheritance, for each of us.

And thank you for "learned," but I'm not that in any systematic, scholarly way. I am a lore-collector. And sometimes, as we lore-collectors tend to be, an improviser, adapter, distorter. In the "unfathomable matrix" of history, culture on the scale of one life or of a people or a country or the whole world, we lore-collectors can be of some use, I hope, along with the true scholars, the scientists, administrators . . . *et alia*!

The beauty and meaning of culture, along with the horror and stupidity: for me, all part of a "matrix" that is real but largely "unfathomable." The art I love and aspire to manages to include a sense of the matrix, the horror along with the beauty, and sometimes the great drama of a struggle or dance among All Of The Above. Parker, for example.

AK: What is your history with the song, "Ginza" (or "Ginza Samba")?

RP: The little tune appears on the album *Val Tjader and Stan Getz*. Frankly, it's charming, catchy, but not a great, memorable track . . . I love the title, the hybrid or syncretizing of Tokyo and Brazil, in the tune played by a bunch of American Swedes and Jews and African-Americans, with a Latin sound. Composed, it says here, by the pianist on the date, Vince Guaraldi. I like the mixing, as I tend to distrust purity.

The music itself, jazz and its family of musics, is syncretic, African and Caribbean rhythms, European marching band instruments, all sorts of tunes and harmonies and weird scales, all with their origins and impurities and discoveries.

AK: I am guessing that some readers will have experienced a little shock that a white man would conjure so confidently with the historical horrors of slavery on the way to a celebration of jazz. Was there blowback when you wrote this poem, which I gather was about 20 years ago? Do you think that cultural headwinds would make it more difficult for a white man to write about these topics just this way, today? Or maybe I should say, a white man who isn't you—"Gulf Music," written over ten years later, conjures again with this material, though in a lighter way.

RP: Here's how I look at it. My notion of culture, of the world, is based on that idea of a birthright that in Baldwin's words is "vast, connecting me to all that lives, and to everyone, forever." But as he says you cannot claim the birthright except through accepting the inheritance which is "particular, limited and limiting."

So if I want to talk about the difference between the three main kinds of Vietnamese language— Northern, Southern and Central— I speak as a white, lower-middle-class Jewish male from New Jersey, getting on in years. And that inheritance is my avenue or window, it is the limitation through which I approach this, whether I am a great scholar of the Vietnamese language or just talking through my hat. So I try to talk about jazz, or slavery, as who I am, with sensitivity regarding who I am not.

I am not a young, gay Dominican-American woman who grew up in Alaska. But what if I have a close friend who is young, gay, a woman, Dominican-American, from Alaska. I read her poems and she reads mine. We discuss our lives and many things together, lovingly. Am I not, to some tiny degree, a gay young Dominican and Alaskan woman? Say, .001%? And is she not just a tiny bit, by her birthright, although through her inheritance, an old Jewish guy from New Jersey?

If not, then what is the point of all this poetry, this reading and talking and thinking?

AK: Among the non-poetry books you've written is your extraordinary meditation on the life of the Biblical David (youthful slayer of Goliath, later King David). As a sustained effort to wrest a blessing from the spirit of Jewish history, scripture and myth, the book is extraordinary in its intensity, integrity, and dogged wonder. As poets do when writing successful poetry, you make strange the stories we thought we knew.

How did you come to write this book?

RP: *The Life of David* is the only book I've written at someone else's suggestion. Jonathan Rosen, a wonderful writer and editor, was starting a series for Nextbook/Schocken of Jewish lives. He invited me to write the first book in the series, about David.

I protested that I didn't have knowledge of the subject, that I had never studied Torah or the Bible, that I knew no Hebrew, that I had left my nominally Orthodox upbringing behind me, long ago, that I practiced no religion.

Jonathan said none of that mattered. This was not a scholarly series, but a series of writers responding to specific lives. (They went on to include Sherwin Nuland on Maimonides and Douglas Century on Barney Ross.) After declining at first, I couldn't resist Jonathan's persistence . . . and, the realization that David's life is maybe the most remarkable, many-sided one ever lived or made up. A great killer, a great poet, a trickster and a lover, a king and an outlaw, etc.

AK: The book honors the traditions of Jewish scholarship with strenuous inquiry that grapples with textual and moral difficulties rather than glossing them over. As a non-rabbi and non-historian delving deep into Jewish sources, did you meet any resistance? How was the work received by specialists and by the broader reading public?

RP: I learned a lot from writing that book— from generous scholars and from great works like Louis Ginzberg's monumental *Legends of the Jews*. Thanks partly to Jonathan's guidance, the book was well-received, both in the general literary way and in the world of Jewish publications.

As you suggest, the Jewish tradition of questioning, arguing, analyzing may have protected my quite non-doctrinal approach, based on marveling at the Biblical Samuel I and II and at the legends compiled by Ginzberg. A paraphrase of the book would be "Wow! What a story!" My conscious model for the style was certain parts of William Faulkner's *The Hamlet*.

On the other hand, at a talk based on the book, an ardent rabbi denounced me, vigorously, for even mentioning the speculation of a homosexual relationship between David and Jonathan.

AK: Did you find that your work on this book affected your poetry, as you were writing it and subsequently?

RP: My way of working is so unsystematic, almost superstitiously intuitive, that such questions are hard for me— everything I'm doing at any time seems to influence and be influenced by everything else, and I have always had trouble recalling what preceded what: in life as well as art!

Andy, I don't mean to be coy, nor complacent about how I work and think: for good or ill, it's all a mish-mosh. Sometimes a diverting or engaging mish-mosh, for me . . . and sometimes, just a mish-mosh.

AK: You said something striking when you were beginning the second year of your stint as the nation's Poet Laureate: "Most every poem I've written is about the same thing: we live in a haunted ruin." I don't know if you had already written "The Haunted Ruin" when you said that (the poem appears in *Jersey Rain*, published by Farrar, Straus and Giroux in 2000). Here is the full text of that poem:

The Haunted Ruin

Even your computer is a haunted ruin, as your
Blood leaves something of itself, warming
The tool in your hand.

From far off, down the billion corridors
Of the semiconductor, military
Pipes grieve at the junctures.

This too smells of the body, its hot
Polymers smell of breast milk
And worry-sweat.

Hum of so many cycles in voltage,
Carbon-fed. Sing, wires. Feel, hand. Eyes,
Watch and form

Legs and bellies of characters:
Beak and eye of A. Serpentine hiss
S of the foregoers, claw-tines

Of E and of the claw hammer
You bought yesterday, its head
Tasting of light oil, the juice

Of dead striving—the haft
Of ash, for all its urethane varnish,
Polished by body salts.

Pull, clawhead. Hold, shaft. Steel face,
Strike and relieve me. Maker's
Voice audible in the baritone

Whine of the handsaw working,
Last harbor of long-dead names of
Adana or Vilna. Machine-soul.

Certainly the mood and especially the pacing here are different from
the poems quoted earlier: more subdued than ecstatic, meditative,
even mournful. While the three-line stanza form is familiar, the lines
are shorter, with many more full stops, with terse commands, laconic
interjections. As an elegy, the poem chooses a breathtakingly unlikely
point of entry, a computer, noting how even our microscopic sheddings
on human tools make of every artifact—even one we are using at the
moment—a haunted ruin.

These tools, complex and simple, evoke the dead of distant cities
and presumably distant eras: Adana of ancient Anatolia, in Turkey,
reputed to have been Jewish in antiquity; or Vilna, also Vilnius, where
Lithuanian Jews were destroyed in the Holocaust. The terse ending,
"Machine-soul," sounds chilling and severe, until one realizes that it's
not the soul being mechanized, but the machine (tool) acquiring some-
thing like a soul, rubbed into it by human contact, and perhaps by the
human intention the tool embodies.

Can you say more about how you came by the sense of the world
as a haunted ruin? Did you intuit something like this even when you
were a boy? Has your feeling about the ruins or the haunting changed
over time?

RP: My father and mother met at Long Branch High School, where I
later had some of the same teachers, as did my brother and sister, aunts
uncles, cousins. My one grandfather had a well-known bar in Long
Branch, where he came as a bootlegger during Prohibition. My other

grandfather washed the windows of Long Branch stores. The town itself was a faded resort, visited in its heyday by Grant and Lincoln, painted by Winslow Homer, who covered the summer beach scene for *Harper's*.

When I was a child, a common Long Branch saying was "the town isn't what it used to be." That might apply to a recent hurricane year, or to those nineteenth century glory days. Maybe also in an elegiac past were my parents' own glory days, when he was a local athlete, voted best-looking boy in his graduating class, and she was a rebellious beauty.

And in those days along the oceanfront were immense, gingerbread or shingle-school Victorian summer "cottages": literal haunted ruins, in a way, outmoded, under-rated beauties gradually lost to arson or condo-construction.

So maybe the past, as a wavery, uncertain object for imagination rather than knowledge, played an early role for me?

AK: This interview is running long, but I feel I need to apologize for having scarcely scratched the surface of your work.

RP: Andy, I didn't expect such close, intelligent and informed attention when Mimi Lang first mentioned the interview. I'm pleasantly over-whelmed: thank you!

AK: We're enormously excited and grateful that you will be reading for our series. As you know, a lot of great poets have read here. Looking at the list, are there some who have influenced your work, who you've admired, who you count as friends?

RP: What a remarkable list! A world of poetry, with of course many names personally dear to me. I met Nina Cassian in Romania, in about 1980, weirdly enough! And along with my own approximate age cohort—Dennis, Doty, Collins—and elders like Kinnell and Howard, younger friends like Rosser, Hoagland, Howe—I'm scanning hastily, doubtless omitting names especially important for me.

• ● •

KATHA POLLITT

• ● •

Katha Pollitt's celebrated poetry collections include *Antarctic Traveler* (1982) and *The Mind-Body Problem* (2009), winner of a National Book Critics Circle Award. She has also won a Guggenheim Fellowship, and a National Endowment of the Arts award. Her poems have appeared in *The Atlantic, The Nation, The Paris Review, Poetry, The New Yorker* and many anthologies. Despite her success as a poet, many readers know her best as a pre-eminent essayist and op-ed columnist for *The Nation* and many other publications. Her collection of essays, *Reasonable Creatures: Essays on Women and Feminism* was nominated for the National Book Critics Circle Award. Other collections include *Subject to Debate: Sense and Dissents on Women, Politics and Culture; Virginity or Death! And Other Social and Political Issues of Our Time*.

About her poetry, Pulitzer Prize winner Richard Howard reflected: "So much has happened to the world since Katha Pollitt published her debut collection, *Antarctic Traveller*, in 1982, yet what has happened to her poetry is a fascinating progress of distinction, of steadying insight, and of meditative enrichment. . . . Pollitt's most surprising gift . . . is the proof that primaveral raptures were literally premature, that our high middle ages are worth all they cost, that life's truest poetry is in the second half."

KPS READING: APRIL 2013

Andrew Kuhn: You have written so well and so much in such an array of genres that there's a temptation to take up your poetry in relation to your work in prose, possibly at the risk of not fully engaging the poems themselves, which are extraordinary. I'm going to try to avoid that mistake, but I do want to ask about how you distribute your energies as a writer. Does writing political commentary or personal essays create a certain amount of static or interference with writing poetry, do the activities complement each other, or do they happen in such different mental silos that there's not that much conversation between them?

Katha Pollitt: Politics does tend to drive out the poetry, I'm afraid. I joke that every morning I wake up with a song in my heart and by 11 AM I am obsessed and miserable. If you pay attention to what's going on in the world—from huge things like global warming to smaller things like Disney selling boys' T-shirts that say "I'm a hero" and girls' T-shirts that say "I need a hero"—it is hard also to concentrate on the inner life, the life of language. At least it is for me. Nonetheless I do think my politics inform my poetry in subtle ways. "Rapture," for example, is about what happens when Christian fundamentalists are "raptured" up to heaven. Hint: it's not so much fun to be perfect.

AK: Your first collection of poems, *Antarctic Traveler* (Alfred. A. Knopf), came out in 1982. Its poems are deft, learned, allusive, with sharp psychological portraits shot through with references to high culture. Horace, Voltaire, Roland Barthes, Bishop Berkeley and Wittgenstein all turn up, but so does

> The mad concierge:
> down in the courtyard she twists to the leaves she rakes,
> her black contrapuntal figure
> a crow, a terror.

The Mind-Body Problem (Random House), your next collection, was published in 2009, after literary acclaim, marriage, motherhood, divorce, remarriage, and not least, the women's movement. In the stunning title poem, the poet ruefully reflects on the suffering of her younger self:

> . . . It seems
> unfair, somehow, that my body had to suffer
> because I, by which I mean my mind, was saddled
> with certain unfortunate high-minded romantic notions
> that made me tyrannize and patronize it,
> like a cruel medieval baron, or an ambitious
> English-professor husband ashamed of his wife—
> her love of sad movies, her budget casseroles
> and regional vowels. . . .

The tone here is bemused, and so assured that it's easy to miss at first the strangeness of the figures—with the mind personified as an internalized oppressive male tyrannizing and patronizing the poet's female body. The sexual politics is explicit, but the reflective, confiding, playful voice is what captures the reader. I think that people who know you primarily as an editorialist, particularly on behalf of feminism, might be surprised at first reading by the poems in *The Mind-Body Problem*. It's not that there is anything that runs counter to the political commitments you have made elsewhere, it's just that they rarely seem to come up, at least explicitly.

An exception is "Playground," which addresses gender role issues head-on. In a few plainspoken lines it evokes the isolation and bewilderment of a young mother, thinking,

> Mama! Was it like this?
> Did I do this to you?
> But Mama too is busy,
> she is dead, or in Florida,
> or taking up new interests,
> and the children want apple juice
> and Cheerios, diapers and naps.
> We have no one to ask but each other.
> But we do not ask each other.

The disappointed yearning for sisterly solidarity is painfully clear in this poem. Can you say a little about how the women's movement has affected your life and your poetry?

KP: I think a woman writing today would have to be truly brain-dead not to be affected by the women's movement. Most obviously, without feminism, most of us would not be writers in the first place, or would be struggling as writers against strictures about what women could say in print that are hard to imagine today.

Not that there isn't still a lot of sexism in the literary world: who gets reviewed, who gets reviewed prominently, who gets anointed a genius and who is just very good, how books are marketed (a sepia photo of laundry on a line: woman author) and so on. I was *The Nation*'s first woman columnist, barring a column on what was new in other magazines, and I started in 1995, at which point the magazine was 130 years old, and had even had a woman editor, Freda Kirchwey, from 1933 to 1955!

It's hard to say how being a woman has affected my poetry. But subject, sure. No man could have written "Playground," because he would not have had those experiences. Even if he was the rare man who spent a lot of time in the playground, it would have felt different.

In fact "Playground" is loosely indebted to Philip Larkin's "Afternoons," which is about young working-class mothers in the playground: "Their beauty has thickened./Something is pushing them/ to the side of their own lives." But the poems are quite different, don't you think? His is more a lament for lost youth— the brief exciting high-school courtship that led to all this tedium and conformity. Mine is more about the way the culture of motherhood isolates women, marginalizing them from the larger world and from each other. The women can't talk to each other frankly, as their own mothers couldn't.

AK: The range of voices and forms and moods in your latest book is impressively broad. In contrast to the almost conversational tone of "Mind-Body Problem" is the lapidary "The Heron in the Marsh":

Wanderer, lordless
samurai,

with only yourself for armor,
tell me, why is loss real
even when love was not?

In terms of setting and the manner of address, this seems to evoke
Japanese and Chinese traditions, as do some of the poems in *Antarctic Traveler*. Early in the second collection, this connection is made
explicit, in "The Walk," about the poet's dismay over the city's casual
destruction of personal landmarks.

A melancholy restraint is surely the proper approach
to take in this world. And so I walk on recall-
ing Hsin Ch'i-chi, who when old and full of sadness
wrote merely, *A cool day, a fine fall.*

Do you have other favorites among classical Japanese or Chinese poets?
Can you say a little about the aspects of their work you most appreciate?

KP: I actually haven't read a lot of Japanese or Chinese poetry, but
now that you've outed me, I will! I just was struck by the way so much
feeling is contained so discreetly, and usually the feelings are rather
melancholy. Solitude is a big theme, exile, disappointment, loss, forti-
tude. All things that interest me greatly, for reasons I could not begin to
explain! The samurai in the passage you quote is invented, probably he
comes from Kurosawa costume films.

AK: "Lunaria," the final poem in your second volume, evokes a literal
late flowering, and quiet hope. It is quoted in full below.

Lunaria

Now that I am
All done with spring
Rampant in purple
And ragged leaves

And summer too
Its great green moons
Rising through
The breathless air

Pale dusted like
The luna's wings
I'd like to meet
October's chill

Like the silver moonplant
Honesty
That bears toward winter
Its dark seeds

A paper lantern
Lit within
And shining in
The fallen leaves.

This is a gorgeous poem.

I very much look forward to your reading on Sunday April 28.

• ● •

KAY RYAN

• ● •

U.S. Poet Laureate for two terms (2008–2010), Kay Ryan won the Pulitzer Prize in 2010 for *The Best of It: New and Selected Poems*. Since 2006 she has been a Chancellor of the Academy of American Poets. Yet this great mainstream success came slowly and late. And despite, for example, winning a $500,000 MacArthur Genius grant, Ryan has hardly embraced the limelight. A longtime teacher of remedial reading at a community college in Marin County, California, she only recently stepped down from that post. She met her wife Carol Adair in 1977 when they were both teaching at San Quentin prison. They lived together 30 years until Adair's death in 2009.

Ryan's lean, sometimes wry, rhythmically deft poetry conjures with rhyme in dizzying ways. Critic Meghan O'Rourke has written of her work: "Each poem twists around and back upon its argument like a river retracing its path; they are didactic in spirit, but a bedrock wit supports them." Growing out of what she has called "an irritation," Ryan's poems do have the unitary, deceptively simple lustre of pearls. In *The Guardian*, Francis Leviston observed that Ryan's poems "reliably deliver a jolt or a laugh or both; but further contemplation nearly always discovers more substance, and more resistance, than you bargained for."

KPS READING: MAY 2012

Andrew Kuhn: You grew up in the San Joaquin Valley, in California, which you once memorably described as "glamour-free, ocean-free, hot, stinky, oil-rich, potato-rich." And you've spoken elsewhere of your dad as an oil-well driller and a dreamer whose ship never quite came in. I understand that soon after he died you first started writing poetry—when you were nineteen?

Kay Ryan: Well, yes, I guess the shock of his death required better words.

AK: Did you pretty much keep writing steadily after that?

KR: I was very reluctant, I was truly, truly of two minds. There was one mind which was completely engaged in learning the craft of writing poetry, and was really not ever going to be satisfied with anything else, but there was another mind that absolutely didn't want to be something that was as embarrassing and laughable as a poet. So I was truly resisting my calling, and I did resist until I was thirty. I dabbled, but I made sure that my poems were only funny, or only clever. It just took me a long time to agree to this enterprise.

AK: In an interview some years ago you were describing what it was like for you early on, I guess during this early period when you were resisting being a poet, and you said that poetry, and in particular rhyme, seemed to be taking over your mind. . . . I don't know if you realized it then—it was obviously intended to be conversation—but what you said was itself like one of your poems.

> I had this condition
> of things rhyming
> in my mind
> without my permission.

KR: I see—there, you've got it too! It's a great disease, though. The longer I've lived with it, the more grateful I've been.

AK: So you devoted yourself, or re-devoted yourself at the age of thirty to working on the craft of being a poet—but I guess it would be fair to say that you were not an overnight sensation, as a poet. . . .

KR: I think we could say that! We could genuinely defend that observation, yeah. . . .

AK: I'd even go so far as to say that, at this point, like it or not, you've become a patron saint of aspiring late-bloomers everywhere.

KR: I remember being so heartened to learn about writers who either were just never acknowledged in their lifetimes or received very late acknowledgement. It made me feel much better to know such things could happen, that it's one of the ways things go.

AK: Do you see any actual advantages to having taken the slow path?

KR: In the long run I do. I think it's good to be tested. I think it's good to find out what you're made of. I think it's good to know why you're doing it. After a certain point you've got to understand that you're not doing it for wealth and glory, or dates, because it's not working. . . . I did it because it was the way I could be most excitingly engaged with my own mind. That sounds a little autistic, and maybe it is, but it was my way of thinking, and it continues to be. It's my way of knowing anything.

AK: Certainly one of the things that has been required in that path, in your development as a poet, has been patience—which is the title of one of your poems. Would it be all right with you if we put it up on our web page?

KR: Absolutely.

Patience

Patience is
wider than one
once envisioned,
with ribbons
of rivers
and distant
ranges and
tasks undertaken
and finished
with modest
relish by
natives in their
native dress.
Who would
have guessed
it possible
that waiting
is sustainable —
a place with
its own harvests.
Or that in
time's fullness
the diamonds
of patience
couldn't be
distinguished
from the genuine
in brilliance
or hardness.

[From *The Best of It: New and Selected Poems*, 2010]

KR: I have a wonderful story about that poem. Did you know the cartoon "Boondocks," the two cool little black kids? Aaron McGruder, I think was the cartoonist. My partner and I were reading the Sunday paper one morning and she says, "Read this aloud, Kay." So I start reading it. The two brothers are talking to each other—Huey and Riley.

And the revolutionary brother is always trying to get his thug brother to straighten up, and he says, "As the poet Kay Ryan once wrote—" and he quotes half of "Patience"! He quotes half of the poem! And he says to his thug brother, "So what do you think of that?" meaning the part about the "diamonds of patience." And the thug brother says, "I want mine now."

It was very cool. I of course have many laminated copies of that cartoon.

AK: I bet! How many poets could say that they've been memorialized that way?

KR: I'll tell you, showing up in the funny papers, there is nothing better. After *The New Yorker*, being in the funny papers. And this was syndicated, this wasn't local. I heard from people all over the country.

AK: Another thing that struck me about the poem, besides that it's a lovely piece of work, and that it seems to express something about your own path, was to consider how it would have been received in a workshop. . . .

KR: That's fun.

AK: You've steered clear of workshops, poetry workshops, and reading this poem it seems like a really good call. I don't know if you're aware of how many different workshop rules that you broke in this single poem.

KR: Oh, tell me some!

AK: Well, right away with the title, "Patience." I mean, you're writing about an abstraction, so you'd get skewered for that right away. No abstractions. That's rule number one.

KR: Okay, good . . .

AK: The next one, the fact that you chose an abstraction, patience, that's a virtue . . . I mean people who can write about all kinds of nasty things without turning a hair would blush to the roots to hear anybody say anything about a virtue.

KR: Okay, excellent, good point . . .

AK: Were you aware that writing about a virtue is a scandalous activity?

KR: I didn't know that, because I really do like to write about certain virtues. I have a poem called "Why We Must Struggle," and that is a not ironic poem. It is a poem in which I am trying to say, why we must struggle.

AK: Do you think of yourself as a moralist?

KR: I don't think of myself as a moralist, although I have said sometimes that I was a faux-moralist. I think of myself as somebody trying to figure things out. I'm thinking, I'm just thinking. I'm interested in things that I just barely know—I have a little hint, a little wisp of something. And what interests me is that thing that I hardly know and probably hardly can know. But what I tend to do, I magnify it. I make it big, I say it more strongly, I maybe make it somewhat cartoon-like, in an effort to make its outlines clearer.

AK: You've talked about the poets who you call the "talking-back poets," about how "they get much of their energy from disagreeing or taking exception." You put Robert Frost at the top of the list.

KR: Oh yeah. Emily Dickinson's another one, giant talking-back poet.

AK: Who did you start out talking back to, and who are you talking back to these days?

KR: All the smart guys. And talking back doesn't necessarily mean disagreeing, but it might mean picking out a line or two . . . Somebody I've been reading a lot recently is Montaigne. I'm a late-life convert to Montaigne. I've been reading Walter Benjamin. I love to read Milan Kundera—his essays, though, not his fiction. And I love to read Calvino, his essays. I had a giant jag for many years reading Nabokov. Brodsky—oh, lots of fun with Brodsky. Essays, again.

AK: In a long interview a few years back you said, almost in passing, that you didn't read poetry. Is that really so?

KR: It's pretty much so, and it's quite embarrassing. I hate to have to confess, repeatedly.

AK: So to continue the cross-examination, when did you stop reading poetry?

KR: Certainly I read it as a young adult. When I was trying to get my chops, when I was in college, I got a BA and a Masters in English literature, and I read a lot of poetry. When you're trying to learn your craft, you really have to be doing a lot of reading. I probably continued reading poetry until I was forty.

I'm not saying that I don't read it now at all, because I certainly do. I've been reading Tranströmer, Zbigniew Herbert—I'm always reading, but what I mean is, I don't keep up with current writers at all. I read my favorites. I kind of went on an Emily Dickinson jag, not too long ago.

AK: Returning to her, because I understand she was one of your initial big influences.

KR: Oh, absolutely. Although Hopkins was the first poet that made me understand what poetry could really do. . . . Brodsky talks about poetry being the great mental accelerator and that's what I came to understand when I was about eighteen—that it really was a terrific brain thrill, to read, say, Hopkins.

AK: Your poems a lot of times have the kind of sonic denseness of Hopkins.

KR: Oh, well, thank you very much. I think the poems play with a lot of different tonal registers. They can be very flat, or they can have more curlicues—they can be more ripple-y.

AK: It was a contrarian sort of thing to be rhyming when you started writing poetry, and even now in a workshop you'd probably get some grief for how you handle rhyme—there's too much for the free-verse partisans, and it's too unpredictable for a lot of rhyming poets. But another way that you've been a contrarian, not just in your writing but how you live, is to come down very firmly on the side of sanity and temperance and not spilling your guts in print.

KR: Isn't that amazing? Imagine that somebody has to affirm those things. It seems like those would be givens.

AK: I guess you didn't go in so much for Robert Lowell and Anne Sexton and Sylvia Plath. . . .

KR: No, not at all, not really. I admire their power, I admire their craft, their excellence. I didn't pay too much attention to Lowell, but I looked at Anne Sexton some, and she can really wield a metaphor, she just has a terrific natural power. Unfortunately other people try to do that kind of thing and they write crap.

AK: How about the late Adrienne Rich?

KR: I certainly admired her when I was in my thirties, and I respect her very much. I couldn't say that in any way she was an influence, other than being a woman poet who didn't give up, who found her own voice, and in human terms was a wonderful, strong model of independence and artistic integrity, following her own path. . . . We all have styles to which we incline, or which are important for us to learn from, and others that aren't.

AK: You wrote at one point that "feelings, attached feelings, are dead weight in a poem. Poems are to liberate our feelings rather than to bind them. If a poem sticks you to it, it has failed." And yet your poems really do stick, I mean you make them stick.

KR: They might stick in your head, but they don't make you feel stuck. I hope they would stick in your head, because really don't we consider the definition of poetry to be "memorable language"?

But I don't want a reader to feel trapped, or reduced, or burdened for having read something I wrote. I hope that you the reader will have a little more available energy. And feel sort of more like yourself.

You know how sometimes you'll read something, and while you're reading it the main part of you is thinking your own thoughts? And you consider it some of the most exciting reading that you do. I remember reading Milan Kundera essays, I was out at a beach—I can picture just where—and it was like my mind was going off on its own, having so much fun. I was closely reading the essays, but my mind was very busy with its own independent thoughts. Does that happen to you?

AK: Oh yeah. Do you have the experience of reading something and you start to feel almost a linguistic unrest in yourself, and you reach a point where you think, o-*kay* I've got to put this book down and pick up a pad right now?

KR: Yes, yes. I have my favorite books, and I can use them. . . . Maybe it's the way that some people use pornography, flip to a certain page . . . I might just read a paragraph or two. It just gets my brain up to speed, to read somebody really smart. To be in the company of Hannah Arendt, talking about Walter Benjamin, it does your brain a lot of good. It puts you in good company, it reminds you that there are some standards here.

AK: And it gives you permission to use high language.

KR: Yes. It gives you permission to be smart, to remember that there really is an ongoing world, of the dead and the living, an ongoing conversation that's really a thrilling one.

AK: We're both old enough to have experienced what a big deal it was when even Wite-Out and electric typewriters came on the scene. . . .

KR: Oh yeah, Wite-Out . . . and remember the tape you'd put in and type over, for corrections?

AK: And the cartridges.

KR: Those were pretty late.

AK: Has word processing made any real difference to how you write poetry?

KR: Well, I mourn the loss of the electric typewriter. It sounds like you remember when there were good electric typewriters.

AK: There was the IBM Selectric, there was . . .

KR: I had a Silver Reed, oh God it was a great typewriter. I could compose on the typewriter because it was easy to strike out, or to write above, and change the margins, so I could really write drafts on a typewriter. But then typewriters became like half computers, and the page wasn't visible, really—where the key was striking was buried someplace down in the typewriter, and it became completely impossible for me.

When my Silver Reed died, I couldn't replace it. And I thought, well, I'll try the computer, the word processor, but I could not do it. I have really bad handwriting, and it was much nicer if I could type, but I couldn't do it, because when you change your mind, when you erase things—they're gone. I couldn't bear for things to be gone because I didn't know that I wasn't going to need them still. That might have been the good stuff, there's no telling. I need all my messed-up drafts. So I had to go back to just yellow tablet, and that's what I've done, ever since the computer took over. It compelled me backwards.

AK: Back to the pencil.

KR: Well, pen.

AK: Shortly after you accepted the appointment to be Poet Laureate, you said you wouldn't be writing poetry while you had the job, and as it happened you accepted a re-appointment, so it lasted a couple of years. Did it turn out in fact that you didn't write that whole time?

KR: Well, I wrote a little bit. But also the death of my partner coincided with that time, and so it was a terribly, terribly difficult time for me.

AK: I can imagine. Or I can try to imagine.

KR: Yeah, don't even try. Just hope it doesn't happen to you.

AK: You were with her for thirty-plus years.

KR: Yes. It was a terrible blow.

AK: I know that she was a devoted and a gifted teacher. Her name was Carol Adair.

KR: Carol Adair, a really gifted teacher. For her, teaching was a genuine art—in the way that writing poems is my art, teaching is her art.
    Thinking about that, about her work and mine, pushed me to try to figure out just what an art is. And I've come around to thinking that an art is something that, when you do it, it nourishes you, it gives you

more energy than it takes away. You want to do it more. It feeds you. It's something to which you bring everything that happens in your life. Every experience feeds into your art. Your art can use everything that happens to you. And you never get tired of trying to refine it—you're never through with it. You never reach the point where you say, "That's done." Maybe a piece of it's done, but it always interests you to do it a different way, and do it more.

AK: I know that your last project together with Carol was selecting poems for *The Best of It: New and Selected Poems* (Grove Press, 2010).

KR: And that was interrupted by her death. She wasn't able to finish helping me to do that. That was very tough. I put the project aside for a while and then I took it up again.

AK: You've described her as, besides your life partner, as your lifelong editor. She read everything before you sent it out. Was she the one person whose opinion most mattered to you?

KR: It's true. Now I don't show it to anybody. I just have to decide on my own, if it's worthy.

AK: Has it changed the feeling and the process of writing for you, since she's been gone?

KR: Ahh, you know I profoundly miss having her to read the work. In many other ways I miss her too, but in terms of my writing, I do miss her.

I didn't talk to her about the work. I would let piles of it gather up, and maybe once a month I'd say, "I've got a couple of poems I'd like to show you," and I'd show them to her—several. She was really a tough reader, she would certainly tell me when she was thrilled, and she would tell me when there was a problem.

And I just hated problems. I only gave her things that I considered finished, and I just wanted to hear what she thought. But I just hated it when she would send me back to the drawing board. And she would. She'd say, "You know, this just breaks down here, Kay, you don't have it in here yet." Oh, God! Sometimes I could fix something, and sometimes I just couldn't.

AK: You wouldn't storm around the house or anything like that?

KR: No, no, I was just kind of personally crushed. And sometimes I defied her. I've got a poem called "Any Morning," it's in *The Best of It*. I was just reading it last night at the San Francisco library. I was telling the story about how Carol just hated the ending. It says "why we / never see it coming / like Hawaii" and she said, "Kay, that is so stupid, rhyming 'why we' and 'Hawaii'" and I said, "I know it is, I really love it." She said, "It's terrible!" I said, "It's terrible, I know it's terrible. I love it!" We just had to agree to disagree on that one.

Sometimes she thought that I insisted on jokes that were stupid and beneath me. I made her very mad in the early years, because she thought that I was too much of a clown, and that I gave it all away. And she's probably right—I preferred to be funny.

AK: Was that sort of easier, at that point?

KR: Yes, I was more protected. Being funny is good, because when people laugh, you know what effect you're having. You live in a nice, safe world.

AK: They're having a good time, you're having a good time . . .

KR: Everybody's having a good time. The other emotional responses are less easily read.

AK: You think having her as a reader all those years kind of helped move you . . .

KR: Oh, she kept my feet to the fire, shall we say. She wanted and required the best of me. She wouldn't let me be quite as lightweight a person as I would have preferred, probably. But she got her job done, she did her job.

• ● •

DAVID ST. JOHN

• ● •

David St. John has authored eleven collections of poetry, and has won among other honors and prizes, the Discover/The Nation and James D. Phelan prizes, a Prix de Rome Fellowship and the Award in Literature from the American Academy and Institute of Arts and Letters. A scholar of music, he has written libretti for opera and a choral symphony, "The Shore." Recent collections of poetry include *The Auroras* (2012) and *The Window* (2014). He also edited the influential *American Hybrid: A Norton Anthology of New Poetry*.

In April of 2016, subsequent to his reading in Katonah, David St. John was named a fellow of the American Academy of Arts and Sciences; in 2017 he became a Chancellor of the Academy of American Poets. He is University Professor of English and Comparative Literature and chair of English at the University of Southern California. Hailed as "one of the finest poetic craftsmen of his generation," David St. John's stanzas of "velvet and intricate suavity" have been praised by Robert Hass for their "intense, dark and silvery eroticism."

KPS READING: SEPTEMBER 2013

Andrew Kuhn: Describing your poetry, Robert Hass has written that, "It is not just gorgeous, it is go for broke gorgeous." But in the decades you have been writing, the kind of gorgeous you go for, and attain, keeps changing. How does it happen that you have been not just prolific, with ten collections of poetry, but protean as well?

David St. John: As much as possible, I've tried to do something different with each of my books. I've wanted to keep certain values about the importance of music and beauty in poetry intact, but I've also tried to shift the angle of perspective from book to book, to test myself, to try out new altitudes and attitudes. I've seen too many poets simply write the same poem over and over, in the hope that their readers will finally get it. That has never interested me. I trust a few readers will be there regardless.

AK: Philip Levine was a teacher of yours, I understand, and he tells a story on himself about being bamboozled by an eighteen-year-old undergraduate—you—into thinking that the post-war British poet Philip Larkin had written a handful of heretofore undiscovered, marvelous poems (they were in fact yours). So you plainly started with something like the poetic equivalent of perfect pitch. Has your growth as a poet involved going through periods where you allowed yourself to be possessed by another poet's voice, and "the anxiety of influence" be damned?

DSJ: Well, that was when I was an undergraduate in Fresno, and it was one of my other teachers, a scholar named Stanley Poss—a colleague of Phil's who taught a British lit class that I was taking—who actually slipped him my poems with the implication they were a group of Larkin poems he'd just run across. These poems were, in fact, imitations of Larkin that I'd written for a paper for Stan's Brit lit class. The previous spring, Levine had introduced me to Larkin's poems, which he loved, and of course I flipped over them. I ordered the English editions of his books and went to school on his work. I also wrote imitations of Yeats and D. H. Lawrence during those undergraduate years. After that, as time went on, I tried to absorb my influences rather than let them absorb me. In answer to your question, after Stevens, I'd say the two most profound influences have been Montale and Paul Eluard.

AK: You grew up in the San Joaquin Valley in California, sojourned in the Midwest, traveled widely in Europe. You are now reportedly again a confirmed Californian, living in Venice and teaching at the University of Southern California in Los Angeles. The American South echoes through your most recent collection, *The Auroras* (Harper, 2012)—as the West did through the earlier *In the Pines* (White Pine Press, 1998)—but so do Paris and Florence. A sense of place pervades most of your poems, even those with a geographically unidentified setting. Does travel help you see the world in ways that nourish your work? Does being rooted in a specific place now also inform your poetry?

DSJ: I'm happy that the importance of a sense of place is arising from the poems; one doesn't always know if that kind of thing is coming through. I've mentioned the importance of travel in other interviews, but let me say again that I do think that travel is—for me, at least—a useful kind of displacement for a writer. It helps to dislodge me from poetic habits that have become unconscious and repetitive. The South is present in large part due to my love of the blues. My poems keep standing at those famous crossroads… and I love living in Venice Beach as it's one of those end-of-the-road kinds of places. The poems from my book *The Shore* (Houghton Mifflin, 1980) sketch out pretty carefully why I love living where water and land and sky all touch.

AK: Your poems have continued to morph with respect to form, diction, voice, tone—you have a career-long record of experiment. Yet it seems that you have pretty consistently maintained a connection if not a loyalty to some pre-modernist poetic aims and values. Your poems are not inscrutable, they embody identifiable states of mind, and bring to life characters with imaginable histories and specific human feelings, although often with tantalizing elision. Grammar and syntax may be stretched but never broken. Fragmentation is evoked, not inflicted on the page. A few years ago you co-edited an influential anthology of "hybrid poets." Do you consider yourself one?

DSJ: I love this description of the work. And yes, what I would call "mystery" is central to what I try to do; yet mystery is often confused with mystification or opacity, which are both quite different in my mind. I actually don't think of myself as being as purely a hybrid poet as most of those poets included in the *American Hybrid* anthology (W.W. Norton, 2009). Clearly, I share those hybrid values in what I continue to admire and love in American poetry, but I think my own work is perhaps more of a combination of Symbolist values coupled with post-modern and highly cinematic notions of art. My poems are also performative in that I think of them as being enactments of consciousness, in language. I hope they might also feel like songs that exist in a tradition that ranges from the troubadours to John Ashbery.

AK: Some of the poems in *The Auroras* achieve a degree of compression that is astonishing, even as they seem to be unfolding in an almost leisurely way. "The Peaks" reads, in full:

The Peaks

Some mornings it's hard
To ignore the chill

Of the nearby peaks
Though the day promises

To be warm once
The sun fully sweeps this

Narrow alpine valley
Where her body lies

Can you say a little about how this poem came to be? Did you start with the landscape, or the human situation, or something that's no longer in the final poem? How did you arrive at this particular form?

Was there a long process of revision, or did it appear at first blush pretty much intact?

DSJ: This poem sits in a sequence from the center section of *The Auroras*, a section entitled, "In the High Country." All of the poems are set in the American West, and I wanted to write something that had a sleight-of-hand effect. I've always loved other poets' short poems, but I've rarely liked or almost never published my own attempts. Charles Wright's short poems from his book *China Trace* have always floored me, but I wanted to do something that felt like my own. I wanted to see if I could pull off those delicate opening lines, those seven short lines, and then try to pull the rug out from under the reader.

AK: Looking over the past readers in our series, are there any who stand out as influences in your own development as a poet?

DSJ: Well, Levine of course, who introduced me, when I was an undergraduate, to Adrienne Rich, Galway Kinnell, Mark Strand, Jean Valentine, Charles Wright—all of whom became mentors and friends—and to Donald Justice, who then became my teacher when I went to Iowa. I later met James Merrill and Stanley Kunitz, who were both important in honing my notions of what I wanted to do in my poetry. I look forward to having my name join theirs in the Katonah series.

• ● •

ALAN SHAPIRO

• ● •

Alan Shapiro is an accomplished and prolific poet, memoirist and critic, as well as a devoted teacher, most recently as Distinguished Professor at the University of North Carolina at Chapel Hill. His thirteen volumes of poetry spanning 1981 to 2016 have won numerous major awards and prizes—including the Kingsley Tufts, Lila Wallace, Los Angeles Book Prize, and Ambassador Award—and been finalists for many others—including the Pulitzer, the National Book Critics Circle, and the National Book Award. He has received an award in literature from the American Academy of Arts and Letters. Shapiro has also written trenchant criticism, collected in *In Praise of the Impure: Poetry and the Ethical Imagination*, two widely praised memoirs, *Vigil* and *The Last Happy Occasion*, and the novel *Broadway Baby*.

Shapiro's body of work offers a vividly lyric account of our lives and times. About his most recent poetry collection, *Life Pig* (2016), Eavan Boland writes, "Shapiro's wonderful and deft volume opens new possibilities for the public and private poem. . . . These moving and powerfully crafted poems make us participants, not spectators. They draw us into deeper understandings of our own losses and give us a language for what often seems beyond speech." In our exchange it emerged that, on top of everything else, Mr. Shapiro is a kidder.

KPS READING: MARCH 2012

Andrew Kuhn: Congratulations on your publication this year of not only your eleventh poetry collection, *Night of the Republic* (Houghton Mifflin Harcourt, 2012), but also an acclaimed first novel, *Broadway Baby* (Algonquin, 2012). Do you sleep much?

Alan Shapiro: I'm actually sleeping right now.

AK: Coulda fooled me. You've been dedicated to poetry for decades, as a poet, first and foremost, but also as a scholar, a teacher and critic. What first drew you to poetry, and how have you maintained such an intense and productive relationship with it?

AS: I came to poetry in the 1960s through rock & roll and folk music. Like all teenagers back then, I fell in love with the Beatles, the Rolling Stones, and most of all Bob Dylan. I had and still have most of his songs committed to memory, and it was impossible not to sing, for instance, "Like a Rolling Stone," or "Subterranean Homesick Blues" or even "A Hard Rain's Gonna Fall" and not become aware of the words and not just for the meaning but for the fun of saying them, the feel of them on your tongue and in your mouth.

It was a short step from reciting or singing lyrics to writing poems, and once I started writing poems I began reading them, and the more I read the more sophisticated my own sense of what a poem was became. I learned to write poetry the same way I learned to play basketball—I watched and studied the grown-ups, the big kids, who knew how to play the game, and when they weren't playing I grabbed a ball and tried to do what I saw them doing, and eventually I learned how to do their moves and put my own particular stamp on them.

Imitation. It's how all of us learn anything. Which is why it's so important to read widely so we have the widest range of models to learn from. Reading is not only how one learns to play the game but how one continues improving, how one sustains oneself. You keep going by constantly expanding your expressive resources, by finding new models to imitate. Fact is, imitation is inescapable. If you don't imitate others, you'll end up imitating yourself, which is the worst possible fate for a writer.

AK: Your early work, in the Seventies, during and after your stint as a Stegner Fellow at Stanford, was rigorously rhymed and metrical, which at the time was even more against the dominant cultural grain than it is now, if that were possible. But by the mid-Eighties, enough other poets had published work harkening back to earlier forms that they were collectively dubbed "The New Formalists"—at which time you took care to disassociate yourself from them, with some pretty scathing essays. Would it be fair to say that you have a contrarian streak?

AS: I lose no matter how I answer this. If I say no, you'll see that as proof of my contrarian streak. It is true I have an aversion to movements and groups. I disassociated myself from the new formalists because none of the poets identified with the group were particularly skillful in the handling of form; plus, in my view they fetishized form as if writing in form were inherently valuable whereas I've always believed that form (and this includes free verse forms as well as accentual-syllabic forms) are only valuable insofar as they help you say something—they should serve emotional and intellectual needs, not the other way around. For many of the new formalists, they seemed to think that all you had to do is count to ten and divide by two and you had a poem.

AK: I've neglected so far to mention that, besides being a distinguished poet, you are also a generous and at times emotionally searing memoirist. Unlike many writers, who protest any attempt to link the work and the life, you almost invite it, in a very disarming way. How did you arrive at this unusually open and un-defensive stance?

AS: Sheer genius? I like telling stories. All writing, whether poetry or prose, fiction or nonfiction, has to be first and foremost a story, a memorable story, it has to be a story in order to be memorable. The only difference between memoir and fiction is that fiction is just story whereas memoir is story under oath. I write to make sense of experiences that are muddled; to bring a little clarity to what otherwise is confused in vexing ways.

AK: You seem to have grown up very much in the teeth of the Sixties, when every personal and esthetic choice was seen through the lens of politics. Your older sister was an SDS radical banished by your father, ultimately for dating black men. Your essay, "Woodstock Puritan," is the only account of that watershed event I've encountered that doesn't mention the music; by the time you escape the chaos and filth—on the back of a garbage truck, aptly enough—the reader is as relieved as you are.

You seem to have emerged from that era with a powerful mistrust of orthodoxies, whether of the Dionysian or the law-and-order varieties. But in your poetry, you continue to honor and enact the tension between structure and chaos, holding firm and letting go. How would you say your experience of this tension, and your expression of it, have changed over time?

AS: Jeez, I don't know. I do think that the only way you can get at formlessness is through form, the only way you can understand excess is in relation to some sort of measure, or norm. I think this is true socially as well as metrically. In *Purity and Danger*, Mary Douglas says that where there is dirt, there is a system. What society defines as dirt indirectly reveals its notion of purity or cleanliness. In the sciences, we are always encouraged to understand one thing in relation to something else, sometimes to that something's opposite. Isn't that what metaphor is?

Eudora Welty says that every story is really two stories and the trick of writing is to find the story within the story, to put one thing in conversation with something else. I'm interested in things in relation or the relation between things more than the things themselves. I don't think I've answered your question, or my answer doesn't seem to have risen to the level of intelligence in the question.

AK: Hardly!

You continue to insist on writing about recognizable people in identifiable human situations, which a lot of current poets, judging by their work, seem to consider outmoded. Is hostility to intelligibility a growing force in poetry now, or do you think it's on the wane?

AS: I don't know. I'm an Old Age guy, not a New Age guy. I think in terms of human experience, in terms of a world I share with others. I'm interested in language of course since it's where much of our experience takes place, but unlike the language poets I'm not interested in liberating the oppressed from the shackles of clarity.

AK: *Night of the Republic* is a haunting and haunted piece of work, it seems to me. You place the reader in nightscapes that are observed with an almost supernatural intensity—empty places still charged with the passage of those who are no longer there. The narrative voice is spare and magisterial in an unassuming way, which sounds like a contradiction in terms but in your poems somehow isn't. Can you tell us a little about how you conceived of this project?

AS: I had to run out one night around three in the morning to get some Metamucil for my wife. I found myself alone in a blindingly lit-up supermarket; I was the only customer in the massive store. The place just seemed so completely strange without people in it; it was as if I was seeing it for the first time, as if I had been a Martian anthropologist come down to earth and was trying to figure out what kind of weird life form had created this place. Then I began to imagine all the public places I spend so much of my life in at night with no people in them. And suddenly I could see how utterly improbable the most familiar things were. Which is to say, that suddenly there was poetry everywhere I turned.

AK: I'm wondering about the title, specifically the Republic part. You're not overtly political in this collection, but thematically and in terms of tone it's about as far from, say, "The Battle Hymn of the Republic" as could be imagined. Is that an intentional reference, or echo?

AS: I was thinking more about public spaces; the spaces that constitute our social lives, our corporate lives. Where we are when we're in each other's company. So while there's nothing overtly political (with the exception of "Convention Hall," which is about how bankrupt our political discourse has become), politics, exploitation, war even does stand back of many of these places—that is, many of these places are the effects of absent cataclysms.

AK: As you know, the Katonah Poetry Series has hosted many distinguished poets in the past four-plus decades. Looking at the list of past readers, can you identify any who influenced your own development as a writer?

AS: That's an impressive list of poets who've read for you. I greatly admire Mark Doty, Sharon Olds, Dorianne Laux, Robert Wrigley, Billy Collins, Adrienne Rich (who was a teacher of mine, as was Galway Kinnell), and the amazing Mark Strand. None of these poets, however, with maybe the exception of Mark Doty, has informed my work in any sort of direct way—the way, for instance, CK Williams or Robert Pinksy, Tom Sleigh or Elizabeth Bishop have, but they are all poets whose work I follow and always, always enjoy.

AK: Thanks so much for talking. We're really looking forward to your reading on March 11th.

• ● •

CHRISTIAN WIMAN

• • •

Christian Wiman has put spiritual questions, struggles, and awakenings at the center of his work. His strenuous engagements with faith and doubt eschew triumphalism or easy resolutions; they address the yearnings of those he has termed "unbelieving believers," people mostly alienated from organized worship but seeking an authentic spiritual experience. A former Guggenheim fellow, he served as editor of *Poetry* magazine from 2003 to 2013. His recent collection, *Once in the West* (2014), was a National Book Critics Circle Award finalist. Essay collections include *My Bright Abyss: Meditations of a Modern Believer* (2013), written after his cancer diagnosis; *The New York Times* praised these pieces as "pithy and passionate, . . . vivid and engaging."

Subsequent to his scheduled reading at Katonah, Wiman published *Hammer is the Prayer: Selected Poems* (2016). A review in *Slate* noted, "Many of Wiman's poems are about faith, mortality, and the rural world he sprang from. Like all great poets, he's in control of his materials and, more importantly, the reader's experience. He sources the right words to help her spot hitherto unrealized resemblances between unlike things. (This is more fun for the reader than it sounds)."

KPS READING: MARCH 2014

Andrew Kuhn: For the past eight or ten years you have been living at a pitch of intensity—and writing out of it and writing about it, in poetry and prose—that few people could sustain even for a fraction of that time. During a period of increasing worldly success, you describe having had an almost Dante-like experience of realizing that you had lost your way, lost connection with whatever had given meaning to life and to writing poetry for you.

Then, in relatively quick succession, you fell in love, learned that you had an incurable cancer, and were, for want of a better term, born again into the Christian religion. In essays you have reflected eloquently and movingly on these personal transformations. Could you say a little about how they have changed your experience of poetry—the place it has in your life, the meanings available to you through engagement with it?

Christian Wiman: Honestly, my relationship with poetry is as fraught and conflicted as ever. I want it to leave me alone, I want to be possessed by it. I want to be known as a poet, I want to be anonymous. If I look back at the poems in my first two books, it seems clear that very little has changed in terms of intensity and even subject matter: even then I was obsessed with transcendence, obsessed with God. I would say that now I don't rely on poetry for all of the meaning in my life, which of course it can't provide. That has eased the mental strain somewhat and opened me up to different tones and subjects. But poetry remains the dark matter of my life.

AK: You grew up in West Texas, and as you tell it chose a college by one criterion—furthest from West Texas. Yet, fortunately for your readers, it hasn't proved as easy as all that to get away.

"The Long Home" is an lengthy, elegiac poem that unfolds like a novella, telling an entire decades-long life story from the point of view of the narrator, a farm girl and woman and wife in West Texas. It evokes the land with extraordinary beauty even as it describes a harsh and sometimes brutal place. It is an absolute tour de force, forty pages of sustained high language that is so fluent and subtly metered that the reader is entirely willing to believe not only in the woman's experience, but that she would express it to herself in just this way. Here's the beginning of a description of the family's riding out a tornado in their farmhouse cellar.

> Down in the cellar where our small light died
> In nooks and in the air behind us—steps
> Ascending out of sight, the far walls gone—
> We heard the first loud gust, a hard crack
> And wake of quiet, like a bolt of cloth
> Torn clean in two. Tom whispered something lost.

Could you say a little about how you came to write this poem, the process of it, the decisions you made about form and meter and narrative shape? And who is J.C.W., to whom you dedicated the poem?

CW: J.C.W. is my grandmother, Josie Clorine Wiman. In my mid-twenties I lived for a while in a trailer in her backyard in Colorado City, Texas. I was broke and had nowhere to go and she took me in. She lived with her sister, Sissy, who like my grandmother was old and failing and spent much of her time just watching television.

Their past became a way for us to communicate. I thought I was doing them a favor by asking them questions in between my reading of the Harvard Classics. (The library had virtually no books, but they did have the entire set of the Harvard Classics, which I dutifully made my way through in the afternoons after spending the mornings writing.) Of course it turned out they were giving me my real education.

One day I came in from a run and wrote down the first line of the poem. That's it, just one line. Then I sat back for a second, looked around the tiny little trailer filled with my great-grandmother's things (she had lived there before her death), and everything just exploded in front of me. I spent an hour trying to write down all of the lines and images that were coming to me, then spent the next four years trying to figure out where all of that material fit into the poem. It was like a graduate degree in experience, which is good since I never managed to get any other kind of degree.

I'm touched that you like the poem. I can't read it anymore. I had an ear and eye already at that time, but I had an inchoate formal sense, and I feel that limitation too acutely to turn back to the poem at all. (Once I tried to revise it with just this notion in mind: that I could "fix" its formal deficiencies. Complete disaster.)

AK: Poetry that is taken seriously has for a long time been largely irreligious, if not frankly hostile to religion. I could imagine that at this point, in America, for a well-known poet and editor of poetry (you steered the magazine *Poetry* for a number of years, quite successfully), coming out as a serious Christian could create more turbulence or controversy than coming out as almost anything else one might declare oneself to be. Has that in any way been an issue for you? Has anything about people's response surprised you?

CW: I've had nothing but overwhelmingly positive response. I mean, there's been the pissy review here and there, but that's always going to happen. And I'm sure there are plenty of poets out there who mock me, but I don't ever hear about it. What I have been overwhelmed by is the positive response from people outside of the poetry world (to the prose book, I mean). Not a day goes by that I don't get a letter from someone from some part of the world who has just read the book.

We all have such hunger to have our spiritual experience ratified, to see our faith reflected back to us by the mirror of faith in someone else. This is always true, but it's especially true now when belief is under siege. My own feeling is that poets are on the side of faith, never against it. They may have no patience for religion (I have little myself) but I'm with George Steiner in that a poem is always a "wager on transcendence."

I don't believe it's possible to be a scientific materialist and a poet, so when a poet like Don Paterson—whose work I adore, I should say— declares that he has "converted" to scientific materialism (see his versions of Rilke) I have to conclude that he and I have very different definitions of what scientific materialism is and entails.

AK: One of the many striking things about your engagement with spiritual and specifically religious issues (faith, especially) is your frankness about still not knowing, about the ongoing struggle involved. You write that besides the fact that Christianity was the religion that you grew up in (and wandered out of for many years) it is the moment of doubt and despair suffered by Jesus on the Cross that has made Christianity, among all religions, compelling for you.

Could you say a little about how you experience that tension between the felt presence and the felt absence or distance of god, and how you manage it personally? [*Note: In the interview questions as written, god was not capitalized, following Christian Wiman's punctuation in his essays. His responses here, however, do capitalize God. The inconsistency is left in place, as it reflects his own varying practice.*]

CW: I don't manage it very well. But it has been a great help to be at the Institute of Sacred Music and Yale Divinity School. These students are brilliant, and they are all fighting for their faith in ways that I understand, and they are doing it under the assumption that "Christ plays in ten thousand places, / Lovely in limbs, and lovely in eyes not his, / To the father through the features of men's faces." We need each other in order to believe, in other words. This is the first time in my life where I have felt that I was in a spiritual environment that I understood and responded to.

Who knows, maybe the whole idea of "the absence of God" is an idol, an anxiety we cling to because it means we don't ever have to act. "Only he who obeys believes," says Dietrich Bonhoeffer, which properly reverses the terms. You don't wait until God reveals himself before doing what he wants you to. You do what he wants you do in order that you may experience God. But how the hell do I know what he wants me to do, we all scream. We know. We always know.

AK: As far back as 1995, long before you came back to an active or conscious engagement with religion, you made the comparison between a poet who is between poems, in a fallow period, and a religious person experiencing the withdrawal of god. Does religious experience now mediate the way the impulse to write poetry happens for you? Do religious frames of reference energize and inform the process, or do they sometimes have an inhibiting effect, or both?

CW: Neither. See above. I just don't feel that my relationship with poetry—with the act and agony of creating it—has fundamentally changed. I don't have a "religious frame of reference." I wish to hell I did. I don't even know if I'm Catholic or Protestant. I often don't know that I'm Christian, though I do believe in Christ.

AK: Your volume *Every Riven Thing* (Farrar, Straus and Giroux, 2011) was composed since the crises outlined earlier. The title poem engages sparely and austerely but with great emotion the problem of god, which as you frame it here seems to come down to his felt simultaneous presence and absence, such that the very unity of things can appear to be at stake (every *riven* thing). The poet seems to strain to hold things together, partly through incantatory repetitions, which have a prayer-like quality.

> God goes, belonging to every riven thing he's made
> sing his being simply by being
> the thing it is:
> stone and tree and sky,
> man who sees and sings and wonders why
>
> God goes. . . .

The declarative simplicity of the language is deceptive; the line breaks lay syntactic traps that jolt the reader out of any complacencies that might have been developing. Even after accepting god into your life, and the tremendous feeling of rightness and relief that you describe having come with it, nothing about this seems to come easily.

This is hardly a feel-good book; affirmations are muted, contingent, hard-won, fleeting. Can you say a little about the balance between consolation and strain in your spiritual experience? Is there something about poetry itself—or our expectations as readers of poetry now—

that makes the experience of strain more amenable of effective expression than the experience of consolation?

CW: First, thank you for reading my work so closely and for such intelligent questions.

Second, I wouldn't separate the terms quite like that. It seems to me that an honest articulation of strain can be a consolation, as in Philip Larkin's great poem of doubt, "Church Going." Or even "Aubade," for that matter. Reality is no different than it's ever been, but we change in terms of the parts of reality we are able to see, or need to see.

Richard Wilbur says that what you project will be what you perceive, and what you perceive with any real imagination and passion, may "take on whims and powers of its own." We have so long projected meaninglessness and despair onto the world that these things have acquired an agency and now demand oblations. We lay down our lives before them (thus the notion of "converting" to scientific materialism). We write about anxiety and conflict because we think that's the way the world is, not realizing that the world is only that way because we have willed that it be so. It takes a great cataclysm to break this kind of collective consciousness, or unconsciousness rather. Let's hope it's a cataclysm of joy.

AK: Towards the beginning of *My Bright Abyss* (Farrar, Straus and Giroux, 2013), a series of short meditations on faith, you write almost impatiently, even disdainfully, of your earlier poetry, as being full of characters thrashing around in search of they know not what, when to you in retrospect it is clear that what they're missing is an awareness of and an openness to god. Once the issue or the presence or the longing for god has imposed itself, is there a danger that everything else will come to seem trivial, epiphenomenal? Where does that leave poetry, for you?

CW: Oh, I don't think so. "You are in me deeper than I am in me," says Augustine. "There is another world, but it is in this one," says Paul Eluard. "The eye with which I see God is the same eye with which God sees me," says Meister Eckhart. "Love calls us to the things of this world," says Richard Wilbur.

The point is the world is the point. To get closer to God, you often have to train your mind to forget God, have to convince yourself that there is nothing but the bare fact of matter. I would be happy to write a book that never even mentioned God.

AK: In a book centered on faith, which presumably offers hope, the poem "Not Altogether Gone" is particularly startling, in its harsh, even pitiless treatment of the death of a cynical old unbeliever. It seems to echo an anecdote in *My Bright Abyss* in which you marvel at a friend's ostensible celebration of his father's painful last days, terrified and unbelieving, but still sticking to his irreligious guns, as it were. Has living under an explicit sentence of death, even a suspended one, made the effort to come into a right relation to god that much more imperative?

CW: The voice of "Not Altogether Gone" is cynical; I'm not sure the subject is.

There is no "right relation." There are only degrees of wrongness. If someone were dying and had no inclination to "set things right with God," I wouldn't presume to say that they should. We all have our potentially saving *agon*. That it is so ruthlessly specific (your battle is not my battle) I take to be further evidence of providence, and grounds for hope.

AK: The volume concludes with this stanza from "Gone for the Day, She is the Day."

> To love is to feel your death
> given to you like a sentence,
> to meet the judge's eyes
> as if there were a judge,
> as if he had eyes,
> and love.

Here the everyday absence of a loved one becomes a figure for compassing the great, final absence. And the solace sought—to love the judge who has condemned you—sounds enormously difficult to achieve. We know from an essay that since your diagnosis you have become the father of two daughters; in prose, you write movingly of your delight in them, for themselves and as an embodiment of the love you and your wife share. Have you written any poems that touch on some of these feelings?

CW: I have. The entire third section of my forthcoming book (*Once in the West*, Farrar, Straus and Giroux, 2014) is about love and death and how my relationships figure in both. It's a long poem in four sections. Very harrowing, but also, I hope, very hopeful.

AK: Looking at the roster of past readers at our Series, do you see any who have particularly influenced your development as a poet?

CW: I had no idea you had had so many great poets there! What an impressive list. Ilya Kaminsky, Donald Justice, Adrienne Rich, Marie Ponsot, James Merrill, and Kay Ryan are all tutelary spirits for me.

• ● •

A BRIEF HISTORY OF
THE KATONAH POETRY SERIES

by Leisha Douglas, Ph.D.
Poet Advisor, Katonah Poetry Series

How many years and poets does it take to sustain an enduringly important reading series? In the case of the Katonah Poetry Series (KPS), a half-century, nine US Poets Laureate, sixteen Pulitzer Prize winners, eleven National Book Award winners and a host of other renowned poets.

The series began in 1967 when Robert Phillips showed up at the Katonah Village Library with some cheese, a gallon of wine, and a bemused poet in tow. Readings continued at more or less regular intervals, three or four a year, until Bob left to join the faculty at the University of Texas in 1991, when he handed the baton to Billy Collins, who had recently moved to the area.

Billy and I became good friends, and I very much enjoyed attending the readings. After a disappointing turnout at a Samuel Menashe reading, I offered to help Billy with the Series. . . . Little did I know that I would inherit most of the organizational duties due to his 2001 inauguration as US Poet Laureate! After my stints as Co-director and Director, I have stayed on as Poet Advisor, still nourished by my involvement in what I fondly refer to as my personal MFA program.

As Billy Collins aptly remarked years ago, *"If you sat on the steps of the Katonah Village Library for the past 23 years without moving, nearly every notable American poet would walk by you."* Another 27 years in the same spot would have yielded the same result! We indeed hope another fifty years of such footsteps will come to pass, as well.

While our audiences have grown significantly in recent years, the intimate, informal atmosphere of our readings, the enthusiastic Q & A sessions and the convivial book-signing receptions that follow encourage everyone to interact with each other and the featured poet. Visiting poets often comment on the acuity and enthusiasm of our audience. Not only have we built an audience, but also a thriving community of readers and writers. This lively poetic scene would not have been possible without ongoing support from grantors like Poets & Writers, a dedicated group of poetry lovers of all ages and the Katonah Village Library whose generous hospitality has been vital.

Some highlights from our first fifty years:

- Stephen Dunn's reading two weeks after September 11th 2001, which audience members said helped them cope with the tragedy
- The Ilya Kaminsky reading in 2003 moved people to tears
- Many moments of laughter provoked by Billy Collins, Kay Ryan, Ellen Bass and other poets
- An intrepid paraplegic attendee who attended multiple events with a respirator and attendant
- A young mother with leukemia who credited the Series with upgrading her quality of life as she underwent treatment

Given the current strength of KPS, it is hard to believe that in 2009–10, the Series came close to ending due to insolvency. Help came in the unlikely guise of a *New York Times* article by Peter Applebome, "Even Poetry is Undergoing Cutbacks." This helped mobilize the community and the poetry-loving world at large—unsolicited checks arrived from as far away as California! With those funds and the creation of an expanded and resourceful Executive Committee, the Series not only revived but, for the past six and a half years, has grown and flourished. One of our regular attendees and supporters, author Charles Laird Calia, recently sent us a letter that I believe captures the spirit of KPS. He says, "What a fantastic series you provide for the community, an unusual service in these fast-paced times, the opportunity to sit in a room to listen and contemplate words and metaphor that often express what it means to be alive. Keep up the good work." Yes, we will try!

KPS now offers four annual readings, as well as some additional community events and workshops. The Katonah Poetry Series also has a new media presence to take it into the 21st Century, including a web site—which for the past five years has included the poet interviews by Andy Kuhn featured in this volume—a Facebook page, a Twitter account, even Instagram! Billy Collins' most recent reading attracted nearly 300 people, and we are delighted to be celebrating our fiftieth anniversary in 2017, as one of the oldest—and newly revived—poetry series in the USA.

ACKNOWLEDGMENTS

This book would not have happened, of course, were it not for the Katonah Poetry Series itself, which exists thanks to the hard work of many volunteers and the support of many generous sponsors and loyal poetry fans. Co-curators Billy Collins and Leisha Douglas have been indefatigable champions of the series through thick and thin over something like 25 years. Rebecca Rogan deserves particular mention for spearheading the successful revival of the series when it fell on hard times ten years ago. (And Peter Applebome, a veteran columnist for *New York Times*, deserves thanks for alerting the community to the danger that the series could go under; those few hundred words made a tremendous difference).

Current stewards of the Series continue to set new records for attendance at the readings. Co-Presidents of the board Stephen Peeples and Moira Trachtenberg-Thielking; Secretary Julie Nord; and members Jessica Bennett, Katherine Dering, Alex Lindquist, and Natalie Dwyer have done yeoman's work organizing and publicizing readings.

In addition, Moira, Julie and Katherine worked extremely hard perfecting the book proposal for *How a Poem Can Happen*, as did Marlene Gallagher, a former board member. And Moira and Julie provided gimlet-eyed editorial guidance for successive drafts of the manuscript.

Gail Greenstein, Lesley Lambton, and Barbara Chintz deserve mention for their service to the series during the seasons in which the readings represented in this book took place, as do former Katonah Village Library head librarian Van Koselka and current head librarian Mary Kane. Jeanne Markel's design contributions have been invaluable for many aspects of this project, from the KPS logos to a fine-art broadside of a Billy Collins poem.

This book would not have been published without significant material support from Jim Tilley, a poet who lives locally and has been a strong supporter of the series for years. He and his wife Deborah

Schneider also provided invaluable counsel and moral support at key junctures in the development of this project.

Billy Collins too has been characteristically generous in supporting this venture, as he has been with the series since the beginning of his involvement. The Katonah Poetry Series itself has also supplied significant support, in addition to a multiplicity of in-kind assistance. David Klagsbrun made the film without which our crowd-sourcing campaign could not have been successful, and his patience and professionalism were extraordinary.

Pamela Geismar guided the manuscript from its raw state to the book you hold in your hands, including designing the cover. Her meticulous and patient approach and unerring eye have been much appreciated. Leslye Smith took the striking photos of 18 of the 21 poets whose pictures appear in these pages, all taken during their readings at the Katonah Village Library. The photos are printed here with her permission, for which I am most appreciative.

The book's cover is adapted from Larry Wolhandler's painting "Colloquial Humor," used with his kind permission.

I am especially grateful to all of the poets who read for the Series and took the time to answer sometimes challenging questions for a stranger, all in the service of helping readers and listeners enjoy a successful encounter with their work. That the interviews have succeeded so well is a tribute to each poet's professionalism and generosity, as well as to the growing audience for poetry in Katonah and in the country at large.

In addition to everyone named above, dozens of individuals stepped forward and provided support without which this project would not have happened. These Project Patrons include:

Bill Abramowicz /
   Andrea Raisfeld
David Alexander
Linda Asher
Deborah Batterman
Jessica Bennett
Ed Biddle
Laura Bozeman
Scott Brooks
Ann Crampton / Roy Opp
Paul Donahue /
   Jennifer Warren
Jeffrey Lee Erdrich
Beth Falk / Dan Herman
Marlene Gallagher
Kate Galligan
Michelle Gittelman
Jeffrey Gittleman
Stephen Fenichel /
   Carol Goodstein
Lisa Gelfand / Tom Tormey
Joe and Jane Graham
Christopher Greene

Laurie Harden
Tim Hart
Barbara Jones
Jamie Kay / Scott Gutterman
Ted Kuhn
Lesley Lambton
Sai Li
Susan and Mark Leitner
Mike Lombardi
Jeanne Markel
Scott Mason
Desiree Meineck
Marianna Messinger
Alexander Neubauer
Cami O'Brien
Melinda Papp
Stephen Peeples
Susan Polos
Rebecca Rogan
Robert Schewior
Susan Sparkman
Moira Thielking
Catherine Wald

ABOUT RED SPRUCE PRESS

• ● •

Why "Red Spruce"? The Red Spruce is a native North American ever-green tree that took it on the chin owing to acid rain, over-logging and other depredations, but has rebounded in this century with impressive vigor. Its wood is strong, light and straight-grained, used in making vio-lins and paper pulp. Red Spruce forests provide sustenance and habitat for many species, including the northern flying squirrel—a relic of the Ice Age and perhaps an apt figure for poetic inspiration, if not poets.

ABOUT THE AUTHOR

• ● •

Andrew Kuhn is a psychologist who lives in Katonah, NY. His poetry has been published in *Common Ground*, *Forage Poetry*, *The Mailer Review*, *Chimaera*, *The Able Muse*, *The Satirist*, *The Heron's Nest*, *The Ghazal Page*, *Vending Machine Press* and other venues.